Downtown Local

Aaron Cometbus

T0413967

Downtown Local
© Aaron Cometbus 2006, 2025

These pieces originally appeared in *Cometbus* 50 and 53,
Mixed Reviews, *East of Odessa*, and an array of small regional
newspapers under various pseudonyms

ISBN: 979–8–88744–109–2 (paperback)
ISBN: 979–8–88744–118–4 (ebook)
Library of Congress Control Number: 2024943053
Interior design by briandesign

10 9 8 7 6 5 4 3 2 1

PM Press
PO Box 23912
Oakland, CA 94623
www.pmpress.org

Printed in the USA

Contents

When the Cat's Away

IAN LIVES NEAR Times Square in an old single-room occupancy hotel. Inside it's like a dorm—or jail. Each tiny room has a sink, but the only bathroom is in the hall for all to share. The sink must sometimes do double duty, especially when the bathroom is occupied by the crazy lady from across the hall who sings opera songs and occupies the bathroom the way Israel occupies the Territories.

Ian gives the sink a cursory post-piss rinse. What's the use in keeping up pretenses or even pretending to be human in a cave like this? You might as well be living in a van. As an experiment, he stretches his cramped limbs and tries to touch all four walls at once. Three—not bad. Practically a coffin. A coffin with ridiculously high rent and a mile-long waiting list to get in. Welcome to New York.

Through the tiny, grimy coffin window, he can see the morons outside the bar downstairs which once, in better days, was a bookstore. They are on the sidewalk smoking and talking. Yelling or screaming would be a more accurate description. They are broadcasting, as

1

if to a packed theater, all the greasy, petty details of their personal lives.

How can he drown out the mindless drivel that penetrates right into his room? Buddhism? Drugs? Ian does both. He folds down the bed and sits in rapt concentration focusing on the little triangle at the base of his spine from whence all inner power passes. Then he takes a pipe out of its hiding place inside the plastic Pee Wee Herman doll and smokes copious amounts of weed. Soon he has attained, if not inner peace, at least deep sleep.

In the morning the alarm goes off. Ian bangs his head on the shelf and curses. Time to get to work. Ian is a painter. Unfortunately, art does not pay the bills—not even the phone bill. The time and energy he should be devoting to art are instead spent working for somebody else, in this case another artist. A very famous artist. Let's call him Clemente.

Ian is Clemente's personal assistant. All day long it's "Yes, Clemente, yes," "As you say, Clemente," and "On the double, Clemente." But Ian is actually quite fond of his boss, and the relationship seems mutual, almost a father-son feeling. Ian is proud of his role as understudy and perhaps heir apparent to the great master.

Still and yet, when storm clouds gather he does not shed a tear. The skies may grow dark and scatter the strollers on Broadway, but a small smile plays along the corners of Ian's lips. He lets loose a heavy sigh and offers Clemente a few words of comfort as he helps him into his coat and calls a cab. "Do not despair, maybe tomorrow the sun will be back in the sky." Clemente only shakes his leonine head slowly and surely. The *Times* forecasts nothing but rain for the rest of the week—and as the whole world knows, Clemente can only work in the purest of natural light.

No sooner has the great master left the room than Ian is dancing the electric boogaloo. He is digging through Clemente's personal papers, he is leering at photos of Clemente's adult daughters. He is pumping Minor Threat through the speakers and bustling around the massive building as if it were his own studio and Clemente only a temporary guest. All these years of suffering have paid off, he feels. If only the jerks from high school could see me now. My own studio, right on Broadway!

Ian looks at Clemente's latest masterpiece with a wary eye. He pulls a face. Hmmm, he thinks. Not bad. Could be better. He pushes it out of the way and sets one of his own blank canvasses on the easel. Ten by ten, too big to even get in the door of his Times Square tomb. But by now he's forgotten all about that life. Why remind him?

Ian drags the easel over by the window and strips down to his drawers. He begins to work, daubing and dabbing, dodging around as if at a dance or in a boxing match. He's oblivious to the traffic outside, even the prying eyes of tourists in their plastic ponchos on the double-decker sightseeing busses which pass right outside the window. Oblivious to everything but the voice in his head and the whims of his hands. He's in the *zone*.

Does Ian really imagine, in that moment, that he himself is the great Clemente—or better yet, that Clemente waits with bent knee at his beck and call, kissing Ian's ass for a change? Or has Ian found a way to strip away all the bullshit and truly become himself? It is the purest of moments, the kind you wish would last forever.

But what's this? Through the daydreams and straight-edge screams Ian hears a distant sound. He stops the music and stands dead in his tracks, straining to hear. There's no mistaking it, someone is coming up the steps. This is nothing less than Ian's worst nightmare. He scrambles to get dressed and clean up the mess, but soon realizes it's no use. I'm busted, he says to himself. Back to where I started from again. Back to my stupid room. I'll get a job at the fucking Strand. Go back to making little etchings. Well, it sure was nice while it lasted.

It's not that Clemente said I *couldn't* use his studio after hours. But it's not really like he said I could, either. "I'll lock up," I always told him. Purposely vague. When Clemente realizes I've been doing all this behind his back, he'll feel betrayed. It will break his heart, the poor guy. Give some kid a chance and the next thing you know he's using your paints, your sacred space, even wearing your robe and slippers, and pissing in the sink! Some habits are hard to break. Well, he doesn't have to know that part.

4

Still, it would be like—losing a son. I've lied to him. I can't blame anyone but myself. Thank goodness he won't know the worst of it. Not to brag, but the things I've done here when he wasn't around, he'd be shocked. Maybe he'd get a kick out of it, though. I should confess, get it all off my chest. Clemente has always been something of a priest, with those severe brows and that ridiculous necklace. But what am I saying? This is bad enough.

Ian could hear the doorknob turning, someone trying to force it open. Burglars? Wishful thinking. That would be too good to be true. No one else but the Master knew the security code downstairs. And no one but him was so lovingly bumbling as to forget the keys to his own studio nearly every day. Oh, Clemente! But why today of all days? Ian looked outside, still the rain. Then came a sharp, insistent pounding on the door.

"Coming." Ian walked across the room as if to his death. But when he snapped back the lock it was not Clemente, but an artist of much lesser stature who walked in the door. Yours truly. "Hey, man," I said, offering him my palm. "Hope I'm not intruding."

Ian looked flabbergasted. I wasn't sure if he was mad at me, or what. He looked terrible. Eyes bugged out, paint on his face and in his hair. One side of his shirt hung too far down.

"You look crazy," I said, patting his shoulder. "You look like you could use a drink. What's the matter, doesn't the Master have any of that Maker's Mark left in the cupboard? That's right, now you're talking.

Don't mind if I do. Yeah, I was just riding by and saw you in your underwear and figured the coast was clear. Between you and me, you're looking a little skinny."

Ian drank his shot in one draw. He muttered, "Couldn't you have called first?"

I smiled, shaking my head. "Ian, my friend. You always forget that I don't have a phone. Even if I did, you never pick up. Have you looked outside? It's raining. *Please*. I'm not going to sit around and get soaking wet."

Ian was coming to life bit by bit. "How did you get in the gate?"

"Oh, that? It only took two tries to guess the code. If people don't have pets, they use the names of their kids. Elementary. But don't worry, I won't stay long. I just wanted to say hi. Give me a minute to dry off—and to warm up with this whiskey."

An hour later, I hadn't moved except to pour a fresh shot and flip the pages of yesterday's paper. Meanwhile, Ian was back at the canvas, hard at work. We'd shared rooms before, and studios, and other things which need not be recalled. We were so used to each other's presence that being together was like being alone. Ian knew me so well he could read my mind.

"Want some coffee?"

"Sure, if you're making it anyway."

The rain beat a steady rhythm on the street. I felt happy. Ian seemed pleased. Sometimes a place to work, or a place to relax—even for an hour—is all you need.

That and good friends. But what in the world is harder to find?

Ian made coffee the Clemente way, which is to say old world. He fashioned a tin foil cap to cover the spout, thus keeping air from entering and spoiling the sweetness. Ian was full of flourishes like that, expertise which if questioned would lead him into a stormy sulk. Yet mostly he was right. Heated on a flame not much stronger than a match, the water had to be coaxed out torturously slow, drop by drop, until there was enough for two little cups. "To life," he toasted.

"And death." We clicked the glasses together gently.

I glanced outside. The weather had cleared up. In the time it took to make coffee, the sun had come out of hiding for one last stand. "You're in trouble now," I laughed. "Isn't that Clemente coming out of a cab? Just kidding! But I'm out of here. I'll catch you later." We attempted one of those tricky handshakes but bungled it pathetically. Have to go back to giving hugs, Californian that I am.

Coffee. Whisky. Coffee. Whisky. I was sitting in the park watching dusk settle over the city while the two forces fought it out within me. My highs and lows actually got along well, making a harmony. Must get rid of everything in between, I decided. But how?

As if hearing my call, a tall, dark girl rode up and pulled over beside me. "Now who's this cute Jewish boy in my line of fire?" she purred.

Oh, Petra. She even flirted when talking to herself.

She cut to the chase. "I'm housesitting this place up in Chelsea. It's huge. It's fancy."

"Small and shitty is more my style," I pointed out.

"Clearly. And a vacation from that doesn't sound great?" She cooed, "You should really come over."

"I'm riding in that direction anyway," I gestured vaguely. I wondered, where could I be headed in that direction? Luckily, she didn't ask. We hopped on our bikes and into traffic.

I said, "There's a cab stand we could stop at on the way and pick up some Indian food."

She smiled knowingly. "Oh, I love that place. Houston and A."

"Not that one."

"Houston and Crosby?"

"That's Pakistani food."

"Church Street, down by the bridge?"

"No, okay? Geez! You'll see." Carrying on a conversation between speeding, lane-changing cars was hard enough without having to account for every cab stand in town.

We turned on 24th by the water. "Here it is."

"Oh, this *is* right on the way." She sounded disappointed. "It figures you would pick this place. It makes the regular dumps look like five-star restaurants. Too bad I don't have a car that needs a tune-up while we wait."

Instead, she flirted a little with the guy behind the counter, who matched her cuteness with exaggerated stone-faced severity. Not a bad match, but he lost. The smile in his eyes gave it away.

We locked up on a quiet, tree-lined street and took the elevator up. The apartment was nice, but not so nice that you couldn't imagine it was yours and not just borrowed. In fact, I quickly forgot. By the time Petra called out from the next room, "Make yourself at home," I already had my shoes off and was lounging on the sofa picking through a few books I'd taken off the shelf.

"Want to eat on the roof?" she asked. "Or maybe down in the garden? Look at that, an actual carp pond."

Nice, but I said no. You spend so much time eating out and on-the-go that a night and a meal at home is the biggest luxury. I pulled a table over so we could sit at opposite ends, then laid my jacket down to cover it. We dug in. It was spicy and felt fancy even with the styrofoam and plastic forks. Romantic. Domestic. I felt like I should light a fire and settle down with a furry animal at my side when the meal was done. Petra evidently felt the same. "I'm going to the bedroom," she said.

"There's plenty of room in here," she added when I walked by her open door a little unnecessarily slow. "If you want to take a nap."

Indeed, she barely made a dent in the king-size white bed. It looked like an overstuffed cloud with a little Petra in the middle as the silver lining. She lay there with a book in one hand and a cigarette in the other, a low reading lamp casting shadows from the smoke. Suddenly I felt very, very sleepy. Maybe it was the Indian food? I hadn't been in a real bed in so long. My eyelids felt heavy as bricks.

I kept walking, and was soon rummaging through the kitchen cabinets.

"Try the freezer." A Bronx native, her voice sounded most natural when yelling.

The kitchen was without food or much in the way of cooking implements, but coffee there was, and a tiny old-fashioned stovetop perc to make it with, just like the kind Ian had used. I was in luck.

I sat on the sofa reading and sipping at a scalding cup of espresso. I took a long, hot bath. The Empire State Building winked at me through the window, even red, white, and blue lights unable to sully its dignity.

Petra came out in pajamas. "You're welcome to spend the night. In fact, you can just move in if you like. No one would know the difference. Unless his mom stops by, that is."

I turned my head sideways, a look of incomprehension picked up from a pit bull I used to take care of.

"Well, his mom doesn't really know I'm staying here. It all happened really suddenly. He had to go somewhere in a hurry. Had to check himself in."

"Check himself in like mental ward, or rehab?"

"Rehab. Ugh, you should have seen this place when I got here. Dried blood all crusted on clothes that were scattered all over the floor." Petra shuddered and made an echinacea face.

"Used needles?"

"Luckily, no, although they must be around here

somewhere, be careful where you sit. All I found were a lot of empty pill bottles. It's a good thing he checked himself in when he did. I had *no* idea it was this bad. Actually, I thought it was all in the past."

"How can he afford this pad?"

"Believe it or not, he runs a gallery. You know that place on Bank Street?"

"You're kidding. I always wondered how they stayed in business. The rent must be insane."

"Right, well, that's the deal. His mom pays the rent there *and* here. She got them both for him as bait to lure him back to New York, to get him off drugs. Which didn't work out so well, obviously."

"It never does. But how do you fit into all this?"

"That's the weird thing. I don't know him all that well. I mean, I haven't known him all that long. But we hit it off really quickly and things just took off from there."

"Wait a second. He's your boyfriend?"

"I don't know. I mean, I *guess* so. It's not really a word I use. He was like, 'You're so hot. I have to go into rehab, I'll be back in a month or so. Here's the keys to my place.'"

"You moved in before you even started going out? Petra! Shameless!"

She smiled and shrugged, hands turned toward the sky.

"So what'll you do if his mom shows up, introduce yourself? 'Hi, I'm your son's new girlfriend, thanks for the swank pad.'"

"Wellll … *that's* the problem. She already knows me. She's my boss."

"That's how you met him?"

She nodded and flashed her "Oops, did I touch that priceless vase" face.

"Wow, that's a total mess. What a tangled web you weave."

I sat there silently, pretending to take in the whole picture. In fact, I was jealous. I wanted to be a junkie and live to tell the tale. I wanted an art gallery and a flat in Chelsea. I wanted a mother. Maybe I wanted Petra too.

But it was somebody else's life, not mine, and stupid even to pretend. The shitty warehouse where I lived didn't have a bath, a view, *or* heat. My neighbors were so loud I couldn't sleep, read, or think. No wonder I spent all my time in other people's spaces and lives: mine sucked. I wanted to take a big shit in the corner of this rich guy's house, just because I could.

"Sure you don't want to move in?" Petra asked.

"I gotta go," I gulped. "Now."

Five minutes later I was on the waterfront.

It had been a long time since I'd had enough coffee to actually feel high. Every nervous tic was going at once and my cheeks were chewed to a bloody dough. A breeze blew through my hair. The waterfront cops screamed at me to get off my bike, but I could not stop. Pursuing me in their little golf carts, they skidded and crashed as I tore through the bushes and down small stairways.

Just as they were starting to close in from both sides, I swerved into traffic and crossed the West Side Highway at 12th Street. I blazed across town, slowing for neither lights nor cars. Finally I hopped the curb in front of a darkened theater and skidded to a stop. It looked like a good place to piss. Instead, I rapped on the glass. A small beam of light emerged from the far recesses inside, sweeping along the red carpet as it drew closer. Then it shined directly in my eyes.

"Aaron? Hey, I was just thinking about you! Come on in. You can set the bike there, next to mine."

Skip was an old friend, probably the person I'd known longest in town. He ushered me in and I followed close behind through all the labyrinth-like corridors that led to the projection booth. He offered me the only chair. Standing, winding film through a machine with one hand, he gestured with the other. "What's going on?" he asked. "What's the occasion?"

"Well, I'm doing a little study, to tell the truth."

"Uh-oh. What is it this time? Let me guess, we have to ride every subway line in one night?"

"Yeah, and carry on a conversation with someone in a different language on each one."

"Cool, I'm down. Just give me a chance to clean up a few things around here." Skip's enthusiasm was unflagging as always.

"Don't you think it might be, you know, a little late to get started?"

He pulled his head back to give me a scrunched-up expression of disbelief or disgust. "Why? They run all night, right? So what's the problem? Let's see, I know enough Mandarin to get by. Then Spanish, French, Italian I can fake a bit. Oh yeah, English. And you know, what? Hebrew, Vietnamese, Polish, and a little Arabic? Maybe some Swahili? That's just a guess."

"Actually, I was just joking. Sorry."

"I know, I was just talking. Still, it was starting to sound good. Maybe we can try it sometime?"

"I'll add it to the list. But right now it would be best if we could just stay here, if that's okay. This study I'm working on, it's sort of hard to explain."

Skip nodded slightly. I didn't know where to start.

"Okay, you live with a bunch of louder, younger guys who are always building these robots, right? They're, like, fucked-up and robot-fighting and fire-breathing in the next room. So, just a crazy assumption, but maybe that's why you're locked in this tiny booth that smells like fake butter, pretty much twenty-four hours a day?"

"Oh, they're not so bad." Skip chuckled. "They're pretty respectful, really. But yeah, I do stay here late sometimes to study my Mandarin."

"That's all?"

"Occasionally there's the date scenarios, you know. You sit in the empty theater, maybe screen a film you've been wanting to see, that sort of thing. Sit around the lobby afterwards discussing it."

"Strictly G-rated, huh? How virtuous you are with your empty building. Somehow I'm a little surprised."

"Well, here in the booth anything can happen, and of course it does. But that was before the new manager. Now there's no more personal calls, no computer access, nobody allowed with you in the booth. That's why I have to pull the gates down—so he doesn't walk by and see anybody in here. In the old days one of the projectionists *lived* in here. It was a totally different climate as far as what you could get away with."

"He lived in the booth?"

"No, worse—under the booth, in the wood pilings that prop this up. John, he's almost a legend around the theater. Some of his stuff is still in here, too. You find it at the weirdest times, like a sock will come flying out. The old manager, he told John not to sleep here, but what could he do? John just ignored him and would get locked in every night. Actually, that's who introduced me to Joe the dogmatic communist drug dealer, who we call Joe Stalin. Did I ever tell you about him? Well, it's a good story. He lived in the neighborhood and would always stop by. It got so that he would come here any time he needed to break up a bigger bag or make a drop. I had a little scale in here which I let him use."

"What?!" I was confused. In the fifteen years I had known Skip, I'd never known him to partake in anything stronger than tea.

"I go through phases," he offered as an explanation or in lieu of one. I didn't press the issue. I was antsy. Claustrophobic, really. The old anxiety was kicking in.

Perhaps Skip could tell. "Want to sit out there?" He pointed through the tiny projection window.

I nodded my head and everything else. "Can I raid the snack bar?"

We resettled in the empty theater, both facing forward in front of the blank white screen. We were right in the middle, surrounded by a sea of empty seats. The lights were on, as if the credits were done but we still didn't have to leave. I felt a snug sense of peace. I balanced a stack of snacks on my lap while cradling a coffee with both hands.

I thought, I am a bear. A very lucky bear. Warm and dry and about to settle in for the winter. What could be better?

"Hey, Skip?" I had a question. "Do you ever lose track of everything while you're in here? Sort of drift off into a fantasy world and forget there's even a city outside?"

"Well, not so much, to tell the truth. Keep in mind, I've been working in theaters for most of my life. That disconnect with the outside world? You get used to it. You could say it becomes a part of you."

We watched the wide, white screen. Then I said, "Are you going to finish your story?"

"Which story?"

"Joe Stalin. I thought that was leading somewhere."

"Oh yeah. It is. So, Joe Stalin has his birthday party at the theater. In the projection booth, actually. Already, he's alienated a bunch of the counter people by his manner, which is brusque, to say the least. He would march right past them, go into the booth, and start breaking up dimes. It depended on what was playing, but sometimes he would completely freak out. One night there was a film about Milosevic, and he started ranting like, 'Whether it's Saddam Hussein or Milosevic or Kim Jong Il, it's always these communists we're targeting, saying they're tyrants when really they're just nationalists, but the US can't deal with them because we want to rule everything ourselves.'

"I'm like, 'Stalin, you got to keep it down, okay? The snack bar guy isn't really the one to proselytize to. He's not going to join your movement.'"

"Get to the point."

"Here it is. It was Joe's birthday party and I got pissed for some reason. I walked outside with a joint to cool off a bit. The snack bar guy was like, 'I don't think that's a good idea.' Even Joe said, 'You're asking for trouble,' but I waved them off. Come on, like it's that hard to be discreet about it?

"Well, two undercover cars promptly pulled up and arrested me, Joe, *and* the snack bar guy, just like that. I said, 'Look, officer, if you haul us off now, it's gonna be a bad scene. There's a theater full of people in there, there's twenty minutes left on the movie, and I'm the projectionist. If the film ends and there's no one to turn on the lights and stop the film and lock up behind them, who *knows* what will happen.'

"The cop looks at his watch. He says, 'It'll take twenty minutes for the paddy wagon to make it down here anyway, those guys are slow. Okay, let's go,' and he follows us into the theater.

"You have to understand, we'd just been having a

party in the booth. There's about a quarter pound of pot in there. It's covered up, but it's not *that* covered up, and now the cop is in there watching every move I make. It's a miracle he didn't smell it. Basically, the movie ends and everyone walks out of the theater, passing right by the snack bar guy and Joe Stalin, both handcuffed. Then I come out of the projection booth with a uniformed cop trailing right behind me. We get the last person out, turn off the lights, pull down the gate, and then they throw us right into the paddy wagon. We were in a Central Booking holding cell for the next twenty-four hours straight."

"In the *Tombs*," I said hopefully.

"Well, not exactly. Right next door. But you can say the Tombs if you want in your report."

"Thanks! So, what happened in the end? Are you all still languishing in jail? Did you die in a failed prison revolt? Did you get fired and never again set foot in the theater where we're sitting right now, eating chocolate-covered raisins?"

"No, believe it or not, nothing happened. I called the day shift guy from jail and told him to hide the weed. Then when I got out I came straight here, fully expecting to be fired. Instead, the boss was like, 'Hey, Skip, you look a little tired.' He didn't know anything about it. Way later on, when he was leaving the job, I told him the story and we had a good laugh. But, hey, we gotta go now, unless we want to be locked in here all night. The alarm turns on automatically at one."

"When does it shut off?" I asked.

"Seven."

Tempting, but just a little too long. "Which way are you riding?"

"Home."

We glided through the still wet streets, pointing things out to each other. Then I told him, "This is where I veer off."

"Here? But isn't your warehouse that way?"

"Yup."

I went the opposite direction. No way I'd be able to get any work done there, or any down time either. Besides, I had an ace up my sleeve. One place I could call home away from home. One room of *my* own—until they caught me there, at least, and kicked me out. In the meantime, I'd dug out a little hole in the dust big enough for a desk.

I unlocked the steel grate on the sidewalk and carried my bike down into the basement of the bookstore where I work four days a week. Luckily, tomorrow isn't one of them.

Mary

MARY WAS RAISED on an apple farm upstate—a peaceful, idyllic upbringing with loving parents who, unfortunately, were also fundamentalist Christians. They taught her the New Testament in its strictest, most literal interpretation.

But Mary was too curious a kid, too naturally inquisitive to accept anything without proof. She loved solving mysteries and searching for the answer to difficult questions. Realizing early that her parents were nuts, she became an atheist and a rationalist. Ever since, she's devoted her life to disproving the existence of God and disputing every word of the Bible.

Still, she retains a fondness for the book the way many of us do for the thing we hate most. Sometimes, passing her room late at night, I'll hear a page turn and know she's in there poring over her favorite parts. Then the next bone-crushing Neurosis song starts, drowning out all other sound and blanketing the earth in a layer of ash. All ten albums lay on Mary's desk, right next to her collection of Bible reference books. I knock but—no surprise—she can't hear me calling.

Diligently she studies, passionately, but without

bias. A love for facts spurs her on, not any kind of fervor or blind faith. She does not preach or seek to proselytize. She even attends an occasional church event hoping to discover a new, persuasive argument to challenge her beliefs—at least someone who can intelligently debate. So far, she has been sadly disappointed. Even an atheist could make a better case for religion than these fakes! A superstition-free world is just around the corner at this rate.

With no religion, the quality of life will indubitably improve, though without the old and known enemy it might get a little lonely. Just look at the punks: Reagan dies and they wander around lost, bumping heads. Mary laughs under her breath. I can hear it out in the hall during a momentary pause in the music. The walls are thin.

Mary still lives pretty much the same as she did on the farm, growing up. The fence posts of her family's fifty acres are now the few city blocks she rarely strays out of. Our warehouse is basically a farmhouse with cats instead of sheep. Mostly, she stays in her room. True, she does own a motorcycle, but like the majority of motorcycles, hers doesn't work and never will. Its real function is not for transportation but to provide endless hours of fun as a heavy and vaguely macho jigsaw puzzle. I refrain from teasing Mary about it, but only for lack of fresh material.

Ironically, it was Mary's thirst for logic and reason that wound up making her religious parents proud. Applying herself at a very young age to the then-also-young field of computer science, she excelled, eventually earning a full scholarship to Columbia University, an unheard-of achievement in her hometown.

What's more, when Mary arrived on campus she found something she'd never had or expected: friends—a whole group of them, sharing a penchant for science and punk. They'd lived together ever since, in a succession of houses and warehouses leading up to the present one. That was Mary's story, and mine too: How I wound up living with eight punk scientists, in case anyone was wondering. I'm number nine, but at my girlfriend's house most of the time, as any sane person would be. Also, I'm more of a punk anthropologist, if you want to get technical about it.

Introductions now complete, Mary emerges from her room as if on cue. Seeing me there in the kitchen, her eyes get a little gleam. With her, even the smallest interaction is infused with a special warmth. She still seems genuinely surprised to have companionship or any human contact at all. Happily surprised, yet it's clear she could just as easily live without it, and us. That lack of neediness is, of course, attractive—and her warmth, contagious.

We sit together at a kitchen table cluttered with beer bottles and bongs. Sadly, our housemates still live much as they did in the freshmen dorms where they first met. Seven guys—you can imagine the mess, not to mention the stench. The tranquil moments are rare. Only late at night, when everyone else is asleep, is it peaceful like this and can Mary and I sit together, sometimes talking and sometimes not, watching the cats run back and forth or the traffic on the bridge just outside our window.

What draws us to each other, I wonder. Friends, that is—not just Mary and me. Is it similarities or differences that attract us? Do we grind against each other like gears, or gather around each other like camp-fires? Or are we just lonesome, casting around to see who might be a good fit?

Soon, Mary will have to go to work, I know. We sit soaking up the last taste of each other's company. Her job is the same as the rest of our housemates'. The same as nearly everyone from Columbia's Computer Science department, they say. It requires an under-standing of probability and statistics, a good head for figures, and a calm, non-impulsive temperament.

It can be quite lucrative. In fact, their pal Tony managed to buy his own house in Jersey with the profits he made. When he moved out of the warehouse, I took his place—or his room, at least. Still up is the proud collection of notices banning Tony from every casino on the Eastern Seaboard. Counting cards is not allowed, but it's an offense very hard to prove. So that's exactly what Tony and the rest of my statisti-cian housemates do.

Mary isn't quite as ambitious as the rest of the crew. Instead of going in person to the high-stakes card tables, she's content to play poker online, small games with fifty-cent pots and nickel antes. The profit margin is low, but so is the pressure. The hard part, she says, is trying to factor in human nature. Certain cards tempt the amateur player to take crazy risks, especially late at night when most of the people playing online poker are drunk. The gambler's belief in against-all-odds luck is similar to the religious zealot's emphasis on unflagging faith. Both are irrational and set the believers up to be fleeced.

But gambling gives Mary no joy, no thrill. She loves theories and theorems which, through trial and error, can be tested and proven true or false. The untidiness and impulsiveness of humanity does not arouse her. In fact, it disgusts her. This is just a job, like any other—tedious, repetitive, and in betrayal of most of the ideals she holds dear. But it is a job, and she can work at home. Hopefully, with time, she'll be able to work less, as she improves and hones her skills. In the meantime...

"I'd better get to work now," she says. I nod my head. Her eight-hour workday always starts at 2:00 or 3:00 a.m. The cats follow her back into "the lab" as she closes the door. Slowly, I cross back through the quiet to my room.

Three Weeks in the Epicenter

THE NEW YORK TIMES, even in the best of times, presents a picture of the city barely recognizable to the majority of its residents. In a state of emergency their reporting resembles reality even less. In response, I wanted to give faraway readers a street-level view of life at the Covid epicenter so that they can compare, and perhaps prepare, for their own experience.

For starters, it was strange to see people wearing face coverings on the *Times* front page every day when on the street it was extremely rare. Now that has changed and masks are common, though still by no means de rigueur. But the photos of empty streets and boarded-up storefronts present a similarly slanted portrait, playing up public fears.

Sure, there is plenty to worry about, but even in a city ostensibly on lockdown, life goes on. A million New Yorkers may have fled—or so it seems from the number of darkened windows in the wealthier neighborhoods—and another million are following a strict home quarantine. That still leaves a lot of folks to fill the streets, especially with schools shuttered and a large number of people out of work.

"Nonessential" businesses are supposed to close, yet what that includes is vague. Smoke-and-vape shops are bucking the edict, as are liquor stores. Bodegas and newsstands are making steady sales, and so are a sprinkling of juice joints and cafes. A nice surprise is that many bike shops and hardware stores have stayed open as well.

The amount of business and bustle varies widely by neighborhood. Brighton Beach is thriving, with booksellers hawking Russian tomes on the sidewalk and nail salons crowded with customers. No social distancing in evidence here. In comparison, the Village and Lower East Side are like graveyards—though the actual graveyards are full of people exercising and reflecting on their own mortality.

The sidewalks of Park Slope are lined with people, but they're all members waiting to get into the Co-op, queuing up for as long as two hours in the rain. I witnessed a Beatles sing-along on a brownstone stoop. As for Prospect Park, I've never seen it more packed.

In Union Square the chess players are still set up at their rickety tables, ready to take your money. Until this week, the hotdog stands were also doing a brisk business. Each day, another fixture disappears from the landscape as the death toll climbs and the virus closes in. Today the fruit vendors on the corner were gone, though they'd been replaced by an impromptu boxing ring.

In fact, closing the gyms seems to have affected public life more profoundly than any other shutdown, since this is such a fitness-obsessed town. Even a plague won't keep New Yorkers from their daily workout. Now instead of spinning class they're riding real bikes. Instead of a treadmill they're running down the middle of the street.

Me too. On Broadway I got passed by a longboarder with a massive afro wearing only boxer shorts and pink gloves. The smile on his face said, "My day has arrived." A disaster brings out all types, and all shades of reaction, from apocalyptic paranoia to peace of mind. My control freak friends say they've never felt so relieved because everything is out of their constantly washed hands.

Cabs are scarce, but the busses and subways are still running steadily—perhaps more steadily than usual—and both are free. The bus drivers stopped collecting fares, and no one will chase you if you hop the turnstile for a train.

Choosing where to board, however, has never been so fraught. It's crucial to find a seat where it's not crowded, yet a nearly empty subway car is something to avoid, because a decomposing human wreck is often hidden inside. I'm sympathetic to their plight, but wouldn't mind the MTA designating special sanitarium cars for the "walking wounded" until a vaccine can be found.

There's always been speculation about cockroaches surviving an apocalypse, but a surprising survivor here is the subway musician, if you'll pardon the comparison. The plague is in full swing, yet the saxophonists and folksingers are still on the platforms playing their plaintive tunes. The incense seller is still set up in the tunnel on 14th Street, though the place looks like the Black Hole of Calcutta, with bodies lining the walls. That passage is enough to make even the most devoted city dweller doubt the choices they've made.

And yet, it's the way life here refuses to be stopped that warms my heart and gives me hope.

Week Two

Greetings from the epicenter. A capital of culture is a nice place to be, the capital of a virus, not so much—or so you would think. In fact, being in the middle of a crisis may be better than watching it unfold from afar. Death is a drag, yet anticipation is worse, so it's a relief to draw straws and get it over with.

There's a comfort that comes from being at the forefront. While the plague continues its spread across the country, the peak of infection here *may* have passed.

Besides, the situation looks different on the ground than from a distance. My faraway friends call up worried, responding to reports of mobile morgues and hospital ships. Harrowing developments for sure, but they still don't accurately reflect daily life here. Neither do photos of an empty Times Square, since it's a place locals studiously avoid, as central to the life of our city as Ghirardelli Square and Pier 39 are to SF. An empty Zabar's would be news fit to print.

The streets have, however, emptied noticeably

since last week. Union Square is down to one chess player, and most of the subway musicians have fled their posts. Sadly, the "we're all in this together" spirit has also faded as fear takes hold. Instead of cell phone cases, the sidewalk vendors are selling surgical masks. Paranoia seems rampant, whether it's pedestrians keeping a twenty-foot distance on the street, or the alternative media predicting an oncoming police state. Just as important as washing hands, it seems to me, is safeguarding our mental health and striving to keep depression and conspiracy—not just each other—at arm's length.

I remember disasters in earlier eras with crowds huddled around transistor radios on street corners waiting for news. Strangely, radio served just as crucial a need here in the first week of the outbreak. DJs were the only voices offering calm and comfort to the masses while keeping the message upbeat. They acknowledged the public's fears, yet soothed them with humor, kind words, and rousing tunes—and by delivering simple, homespun truths. DJs were the unsung heroes playing the role that government left mostly unfilled.

Which is why, when they too began to disappear it was a very bad sign, the proverbial canary in the coal-mine. The radio personalities didn't die, so far as I know, yet one by one they were removed to "undisclosed remote locations" for their own good—playful wording that had an unintended chilling effect. Prerecorded air checks took their place, with none of the warmth or charm.

And that's the feeling this week in the city that never sleeps: Life goes on, but with hope at half-mast and a lot of the vigor gone. Pets are the only thing thriving in this crisis, as WCBS's Broadway Bill Lee pointed out before he was unceremoniously whisked away. Cats are getting the attention they crave, and canines are being walked by their owners for a change, instead of the professional dogwalkers who shepherd whole packs at a time.

People compare the deserted landscape and boarded-up storefronts to a zombie apocalypse, but to me it's like living in Delaware in the eighties, which was even worse. Still, the city is unchanged in some respects. At 4:00 a.m. bodegas and a few restaurants were always the only places open, and most people you met were crazy or drunk. The change is that 4:00 p.m. is no different now. The city's hidden dark side is in plain view.

The can collectors and homeless are still on every block, but the daytime population is sequestered around-the-clock, and commuters and tourists are nowhere in sight. You can stroll right down the middle of the street like Bob Dylan—even on Canal, a boulevard normally scary to cross even with the light.

The trains I mentioned running with regularity in my last report? They are few and far between now that the MTA trimmed everything but "essential services." The predictable result is packed subway cars that make social distancing a joke. Trains are one of the few crowded places to be found, along with the plazas in Midtown which legions of skaters have taken over since the security guards are gone. The same goes for Washington Square, where the legendary fountain has become a skatepark, and the drug dealers are out in greater numbers than ever before.

Besides the daylong wait outside the Co-op, the only steady lines I've seen are in the Village, and not for the staples you might expect. Grubhub freelancers on bikes queue up at St. Vincent's Triangle every afternoon for homecooked West African meals served by an enterprising woman with a minivan. Here, even delivery guys order delivery. Meanwhile on Broadway a crowd of weary people stand outside the Strand— not to get into the shuttered bookstore, but to line up single-file for the beauty supply place next door. I braved that line myself, and it was well worth the wait. Being called "baby" by the counterwoman may be the only affection I'll receive this week.

Are you ready for some good news for a change?

If you're reading this, you're alive—and it's good to be alive.

And in this normally noisy metropolis you can hear the birds sing.

Week Three

I took a long ride through the middle of Manhattan to begin my week, and this weekly report, with a panoramic view.

On the west side waterfront, men were boxing and moms were dancing with their kids. You wouldn't guess this was ground zero of a pandemic except for the social distancing and face masks that have come to seem almost normal. The widespread use of bandannas has given the city an Old West feel, and there were lots of bandits on the bike path. Some people can smile with their eyes, but not most of the folks I passed this week.

The population of Hell's Kitchen was a bit warmer, made up of the usual split: half desultory doorway smokers and half enthusiastic waving guys in wheelchairs. But Times Square was empty, confirming reports I'd been highly skeptical of. In a five-block stretch I saw forty or fifty people max, and half of them were cops.

The Diamond District was rather lovely in its desolation, deserted besides a few more officers of the law and one extremely animated doorman with what used to be called a ghetto blaster pumping out Latin songs. He gave me what I've been looking for since this damn quarantine began: a cheer and a fist in the air.

The nearby Japanese market was open, the Algerian mission closed. Outside UN headquarters a solitary demonstrator beat the drum—a hand-held, shallow variety I associate with Mickey Hart. "Eliminate the Communist Party of China," read his defaced Chinese flag. A lone translator edged past us to show her ID and gain entry from the security guard at the gate. Otherwise there were no signs of life.

Ferries departed and arrived on the East River, though far less than in pre-apocalypse times. The throngs of joggers, however, seemed just as thick as they've always been. I was touched by the sight of a man running alongside his tiny daughters on bikes while the whole family kept up a marathon pace. The spray of water in the air warmed my heart, like the smell of jasmine in the breeze. Plague or no plague, spring had arrived.

I was reminded of a recent proclamation by our governor: "Now is not the time to be playing frisbee in the park with your friends." Those were foolish words for anyone to speak, but particularly offensive coming from a powerful figure at a time when physical and mental health are essential to maintain, and ways to stay active and social at a safe distance are hard to find. Having failed to deliver the promised ass-kicking of the virus—or any meaningful tax abatement or rent relief—Cuomo made a bold stand instead against friendship and frisbees. He'll fit right in as a presidential candidate.

That was just one example of the government's increasingly paternalistic approach to protecting us. Loudspeaker trucks cruised at a crawl through Prospect Park, blocking joggers and ruining one of the very few remaining options for a moment of peace. Their bleating broadcast was unintelligible despite being blasted at an ear-splitting volume, but a similar warning played nonstop on the subway, seemingly recorded by the same folks who did the voices of the parents for the Peanuts specials on TV. In case we still didn't get the message, huge signs were erected around town telling everyone exactly how far apart we should stay.

The result was exhausting and insulting. Even someone like me who gets their news from anti-social media is well aware of the protocol by now. "Thanks Mayor Bitch Ass" read some fresh graffiti on Fourth Avenue, though whether it was a response to this current waste of tax dollars or something else, I couldn't tell. Meanwhile, the state's largest health-care provider ran ads telling anyone who felt sick to "get rest and binge-watch your favorite shows." Nowhere did I hear the message that this pause could be a much-needed opportunity to get our lives in order, or simply read and reflect.

I'd hoped the plague would lead to a flowering of truly direct messaging, but have only spotted a few examples so far. A poem that began "I have always been socially isolated" was taped to a lamppost in the heart of the Village, while manifestos wheatpasted near Union Square were filled with headache-inducing fine print. Graffiti has multiplied, but not to the extent I would have guessed, and mostly on the handful of upscale businesses that boarded up their storefronts in anticipation of civil unrest. "Cowards" says the note outside the Aesop outlet in Chelsea, though instead of being tied to a brick, it was printed neatly and attached with scotch tape.

Finally, I have to take back what I said last week about the goriest developments not intersecting our daily lives. I hadn't realized that the double-wide semi

I pass every day is a mobile morgue. Still, it would be shortsighted to see myself, and for us to see ourselves, as victims in waiting or the ones with the most to fear. This virus is not chiefly a New York or American problem. As bad as it is here—or in China, Italy, and Iran—it's going to be far worse for the countries that are crowded and poor, not to mention countries like Yemen and Syria that are currently at war. The developing nations of the world have still barely had a chance to find their feet. I worry for them with this new plague. Relatively speaking, we are going to be alright.

The Monster

I WAS IDLING around the warehouse when the phone rang. It was Ian. He sounded worried. "What are you doing there?" he asked. "Is something wrong? I called you at home but the Monster answered and told me to try you here."

I put my head in my hands. Accidentally mention the pet name you have for your partner—even once—and you never hear the end of it. "Look, it's not like I actually call her 'the Monster.' It was just that one time, in reference to the missing carton of ice cream.

"Anyway, I don't *live* with her, I live here. You might remember seeing my room. It's got this huge drawing on the wall some idiot made when he was drunk. Any time you want to paint over it like you promised, feel free."

"I would have come by already," Ian said, "but I heard you'd moved out."

"Bullshit. Who told you that?"

"You did. When someone's in love and having a lot of sex, it's obvious. Your body tells the story for you. I figured by now you'd moved in with her."

I sent a low, angry growl over the wire, a warning to go no further.

"What's there to be embarrassed about? It's nice to see you smiling for a change."

"I *don't* want to talk about it."

"Suit yourself," he said. "You were the one who brought it up."

Was I? I tried to remember the conversation in reverse. "I don't want to talk about it," I said. After he said what? That it was nice to see me smiling for a change.

But what came before that? No clue. My mind was hopelessly jumbled. All the years of drug use had finally taken their toll on my short-term memory. But why did this only seem to happen when talking to Ian?

He cut in on my reverie. "I'll be honest with you. The Monster told me herself when I ran into her at the post office the other day. She said you had all your books and even your bike at her place. She seemed pretty happy about it, too."

"Ian, I'm telling you, you've got to stop calling her that. She'll kill me if she finds out. She'll kill you too. And for the record, I'm not about to settle down like that. I like to live with, you know, a whole community of people."

"Sure, sure. I know how it is. You spend every minute of the day with your sweetheart. Then when she has to leave to go to work—to pay rent on her place where you *don't* live—you get bored and decide to drop by the warehouse to see if you got any messages. Hey, it's an old story. I'm just lucky I caught you there."

I waited for Ian to finish laughing. There was some

rivalry underneath our repartee, but the tension was still an attraction for the time being.

"Okay, very funny. Enough already. Did you call just to give me shit, or do you want to hang out?"

"I *want* to. Really. But I can't. I'm at Clemente's right now—his house, not the studio. He went on vacation, so I'm stuck taking care of the place while he's gone."

"Taking care of the place? You mean getting high and lying around the mansion. Why didn't you call me sooner?"

Suddenly Ian was all business. Even his voice changed. "It's actually a lot of work. I have to water the plants. Feed the monkeys. Stuff like that."

"Monkeys? Come on, you're not serious."

"Can't you hear them in the background? *Hey, shut the fuck up, you apes!* And his daughters are here too, with their kids. So not only do I have to feed the monkeys, I have to change diapers for the little Clementes."

"Ah, the glamorous life of a personal assistant. But somehow I'm having a little trouble believing you about the monkeys."

"Believe it. You should see these little fuckers. They're listening to me right now, watching my every move. I don't know what they're plotting, but they're up to no good. *A bunch of hoodlums is what you are! You don't scare me!*"

"Ian, come on." I spoke slowly, calmly. My late-night disc jockey voice. The Isaac Hayes impression.

"Easy now. You're always exaggerating things. What's there to worry about, really?"

His laugh was brittle. "Easy for you to say. If they were staring at you right now, you'd feel differently. A hundred beady little eyes filled with hate. *Just try it, you fuckers!* I'm telling you, if they had a gun, they'd shoot me. They wouldn't think twice. And who says they haven't got one?"

"Ian, man, quit it. You're freaking me out."

"What a week. I'm telling you, it's been crazy. First, Clemente comes over to my place. What did you call it, 'a toilet, except the door opens in'? Can you believe it, the great Master, in my toilet! It was incredible."

"How'd you both fit?"

"I had to throw away the bed—but it was worth it. He viewed my new work and gave me some advice. Imagine if Rembrandt had an apprentice he was helping along."

"Wow," I said. "Yeah. So what'd he say?"

"He hated them. *The colors are horrible*, he said. *The compositions are terrible. This is idiotic!* He was yelling so loud I thought the woman across the hall would hear."

"You told me she could even hear you think. Your rooms are pretty close."

"That's why I bribed her to leave for the night. I set her up with a tab at the bar downstairs. But he was yelling so loud, I thought she might come up to see what the commotion was."

"Damn, I'm sorry to hear it."

"No, you don't understand. No one understands! It was *perfect*. He was right, of course. That was just what I needed to break out of the rut I didn't even realize I was in. So, I threw out all those paintings. Now I'm finally taking chances. Trying something new."

"What's that?"

"Etchings."

"Etchings? But that's what you were doing in the nineties."

"See, it all comes full circle. That's the beauty of it. Now all my old art school friends are jealous, though first I had to explain to them why they should be."

"Ian? Hey, I'm just wondering, are you putting aside some money? A little nest egg to fall back on, just in case?"

Apparently I'd hit a sore spot. He answered as if hurt. "What? Why would I ask for money for a favor between friends, after all Clemente's done for me? I don't want him to think that all I care about is his money."

"Ian, you owe me forty bucks."

"Sure, I remember. I'll get it back to you as soon as I can. But you know what's unbelievable? You have to hold the food in your hand so they know it's okay to eat. Then you have to drop it right into their mouths piece by piece. You're feeding them, yet they stare at you like you're some kind of murderer. Like *you're* the animal."

"Good thing you're not planning on having kids. Or are you? Look, gas the apes and come over. We'll get some beer. I know exactly how you feel—I've got an anteater and a couple polar bears here and they're nothing but trouble. And not kosher either, according to Mary. I won't even start about the cats. Look, we'll commiserate."

"I can't. To tell you the truth, I already have plans. They got delayed. That's why I called you."

"To waste time while you waited for some girl to show up?"

"More or less."

"I'm beginning to get the picture now. You thought I wouldn't be home and you could leave a message about what a bad friend I am. I'll bet you were even bluffing about the Monster—about calling me at her place. Thirty minutes into your lecture on primate behavior, the truth comes out. So who are you meeting?"

After a moment of hesitation, he answered. "Crazy Edith."

"Crazy Edith, your girlfriend? Or a different Crazy Edith?"

Now it was Ian's turn on the defensive. "She's *not* my girlfriend. Look, I'll call when Edith gets here. Maybe I can meet you later on. I'll see how long we're going to be hanging out."

"What's your guess, five years? Ten?"

"Arrr! I hate you! But I'll call back as soon as she gets here."

I set the phone back in its cradle. No point waiting; Ian wouldn't be calling. Like most of my friends, he didn't want to reach me, just to be on record as having tried. I couldn't complain, having played that game myself numerous times. Besides, I was now one point ahead.

Then a thought struck like lightning, making me shiver. Today we were in an adolescence extended like our student loans. Tomorrow we'd be shut-ins and cat ladies like every other middle-aged jerk in town.

I thought of the crazy woman across the hall from Ian. How foolish to think we were immune. We were next in the same queue!

Well, people are strange. Luckily I'm not one of them. I put on my shoes and stepped out onto the street. Rain filled the gutters but still the damn Mister Softee truck wouldn't shut up. Hello! Hello!

Skip

SUMMER IS THE SEASON when all of New York hates all of New York. And no wonder, the place is a fucking pit—a festering, sweltering piece of shit. You step out on the street and start pushing people out of the way. "Fuck you, old man. Fuck you, little kid," you say.

It's not just an isolated bad mood or a case of not enough coffee in the morning. No, every single person who hasn't escaped is feeling the same way. Eight million matches crammed into a powder keg and ready to blow.

"Get off the sidewalk, shithead," some old bag yells at a bike messenger. "Go back to the dark ages, you fucking idiots," I scream, chasing the Christians out of the park. I lean back on a bench and catch my breath. I watch a pretty girl pass. "I hate you," her T-shirt says—"yes, you," on the back.

Skip arrives and sits down beside me. His eyes are earnest. "Whew!" he sighs. "I'm sure glad to be alive."

I knit my brows at him and a grimy sheet of sweat falls from my face like rain. Ever since his stroke last year, Skip just hasn't been the same. He's turned touchy-feely. Someone has stolen the world's biggest asshole and replaced him with a guy who wants to tell you how much he loves you. Which is nice. But New York in the summer is not the place or time.

Skip waved away my angry glare. "I'm not talking about my stroke," he explained. "I'm talking about the guy on the subway on my way here. These days you can't tell if someone's crazy or just on the phone. This guy was yelling about something—or maybe rapping, I couldn't tell.

"I had my headphones on and kept turning up the volume to drown him out. Finally they were up all the way, and so was he. I was thinking, 'Man, even I can rap better than that.' He sounded like a Sesame Street record. 'Blah blah, got a gun. Blah blah, have some fun. Blah blah, you better run.'

"I was laughing. Then I looked around and saw everyone's expressions. Well, you can see where this is headed. The guy was coming unraveled fast. First he's threatening everyone in general, then he starts getting right up in each person's face. Finally this one construction worker is like, 'Look, if you spit on me again, I'm gonna have to hit you. I'm warning you.'

"So what does the guy do? Spits on him again, of course. And before you know it, bam! The crazy guy is flat on his back. The construction worker is hovering over him, keeping him from getting up.

"Problem solved, right? You'd think everyone would be relieved. Not a chance. They're up out of their seats and yelling all at once. 'Kill him! Kill him! Hit him again! Fuck him up!'

"The tables were turned, just like that. Everyone

44

who had been cowering in his seat is now strutting around like a hero trying to make up for it. It was a total lynch mob. I was thinking how good things had been when it was just the one crazy guy instead of a whole crowd.

"Well, the mob chased the poor guy off the train at 14th Street. Then I had a seat to myself, which was nice—but I felt sort of sick. Sure, he got what he deserved. What did he expect? As if everybody hadn't started their day thinking, 'Goddamn, if I have to deal with *one more* crazy person with a gun, I'm gonna lose it and start shooting everyone.'

"Then this guy comes along. He should have known not to take it so far. So you're a crazy guy with a gun—so what? No need to scream about it. We get the idea. But he was just over the top. Still, I felt bad. I hate to see anyone get hurt."

I was amazed. I couldn't believe how calm Skip was about the whole thing. I tore down the street ready to strangle strangers for walking too slow or talking too loudly on the phone. I threw rocks at cars that blocked the crosswalks.

Even in the best of moods—especially in the best of moods—I dreamed about planting bombs in every public place. Meanwhile, Skip rode the A train with some maniac who threatened to blow his head off and all he could think was, "I hope the poor guy doesn't get hurt."

Skip listened patiently, peering at me through wizened eyes. Well, he was probably just stoned, but still. "Don't get me wrong," he said. "You haven't been living here long if you don't want to kill every single person you see—either that or hide in your room with the shades down, only leaving for appointments with the shrink.

"That's perfectly normal. Everyone's in a homicidal rage ninety percent of the time, and I'm not just talking about the summer. But those are idle threats and fantasies, I'm pretty sure. If they weren't, you'd see a lot more real violence. In fact, it's kind of a miracle you don't see more.

"As for me, I might be happy to be alive, but that doesn't mean I don't wish that everyone else would die—besides you and a few other friends, of course. I still hate the human race just as much as I always have. The dilantin hasn't turned me into a complete vegetable yet. I still have a few feelings left.

"But the doctor told me, 'Calm down or you're dead.' So I'm trying. Keep that in mind. Also, I'm superstitious, as you know. The more I complain about that crazy guy, the more likely it is that when I get on the train going home, he'll be there again—bandaged up and with a cast, but even more pissed. So let's change the subject, okay?"

I agreed. But one thing was weighing on me. If it was so normal to feel violent and angry, what made someone like me so different from the crazy guy on the train?

Skip laughed. "You think there's a difference? You both get up in the morning and he takes wheat toast while you take rye. There's your difference."

Around the World in New York

ON 35TH STREET just off the East River, a red flag flies high. Lights are on in the upper levels but no one can be seen stirring. Could this unassuming building really be a massive nest of foreign communists—an independent, autonomous Chinese mainland in the middle of Manhattan?

It could be, and it is. Cross this threshold and you'd be in China. Like all missions to the UN, it is sovereign territory. United States laws do not apply, United States police cannot enter. But what about me?

I rang the doorbell then sat on the steps smoking. Only a moron would start a fact-finding tour of every nation in the world at midnight, but there I was.

It was too late to tour UN headquarters, where all 192 generally recognized nations are gathered under one roof. Too late to find a citizen of every country among the patrons at the UN post office—with its own decolonization and disarmament stamps—or in the UN coffee shop, where every staffer speaks a different language, making even the simplest order a game of Chinese telephone.

Even the multinational crowd of kids from UN High who hang out on the waterfront at 23rd Street (look for the "UN High sucks" graffiti) had dispersed long ago.

The UN missions—the headquarters for the foreign diplomatic corps—were my only chance. They were approachable even in the middle of the night. But how much could I uncover, stuck outside?

There were lights on next door, and foul but familiar music emanating from the place. Left with no other choice, I took my prying questions to China's neighbor, a sports bar. This place was definitely American, and though they looked at me like I wasn't, I was used to that. I pulled up a stool at the counter. The bartender was sufficiently bored.

"Chinese ambassadors? No, they never come in here," he told me. "They have their own pool table and bar—you can see it through the window out back."

The waitress chimed in. "We had a party once from the mission." I could already see where this was headed. There are many kinds of people in the world, but to a waitress, only two. She pulled a face. "Really bad tippers."

I passed the missions for Malta, Armenia, Namibia. There was no one out. Botswana, Indonesia, South Africa. Outside Rwanda was a minivan with a cracked windshield, parking ticket, and missing hood ornament, but the flag on the antenna didn't match the mission; it belonged Burundi, Rwanda's East African neighbor. Were the ambassadors huddled together inside responding to a regional catastrophe, or just unwinding with old schoolmates over drinks?

Continuing uptown, I came to a building which seventeen nations share, most of them small and relatively poor islands in the South Pacific or Caribbean with one thing in common: they were once British colonies and are now part of the British Commonwealth. The cement barricades and police guards, however, are not for the protection of Grenada, the Maldives, or Tuvalu, but for an infamous entity on a higher floor: Israel.

A block away, the UN mission for North Korea had no barricades or police protection despite recent threats to their sovereignty—and *this* country is only starting to develop its nuclear arsenal.

During the reunifications following the fall of the Berlin Wall, the UN mission of East Germany moved into the West German headquarters. South Yemen, who rented, moved in with North Yemen, who owned their office. Though the motives were economic rather than political, it was the doctrinaire communist side that packed up in both cases. Most likely in the inevitable Korean unification to come, North Korea will be leaving Second Avenue for the more spacious digs of South Korea on 45th Street, so visit while you can.

Right next door is another address many disparate nations share: 866 Second Avenue, home of Ethiopia, Bahrain, Greece, Morocco—and East Timor, which splits a floor with its former colonial masters, Portugal. Surely a story of forgiveness was waiting to be told, or perhaps guilt and reparations.

I scared the few folks entering and exiting the

building, chasing after them with notepad in hand. Each one claimed to be merely a janitor or repairman. On the corner stood one of the last remaining phone booths in town. Portugal had their answering machine on, so I left a mean message. At Timor-Leste (East Timor's official name) I reached a secretary, despite the late hour. "I am not myself from Timor-Leste and cannot comment on whether Portugal's offer of office space was, or was not, a gesture of reconciliation."

Well, what did I expect? Diplomats are supposed to be diplomatic. They're not paid to exacerbate international tensions.

Off the avenues, the UN missions are more interesting, mostly small and low-lying by Manhattan standards, because no country is going to tear down its brownstone to build towering condos. What's the point in having sovereign territory if you've got noisy or nosy renters who could be State Department spies, known to tap not only phones but even the plumbing at one hotel where Khrushchev stayed, in order to analyze his shit?

Unpleasant, I know. But as a result, these missions are some of Manhattan's most stable and settled homeowners, permanently preserving the city's old world, and whole world, charm.

Comparing the different properties is a lesson in resources and politics. San Marino, once the only Eastern Bloc state in the West, has a cottage as tiny as their country. Others, especially oil-rich nations like Libya, are hard to miss. When I passed Libya House, piles of paper were blowing down the sidewalk, flapping like a flock of birds, giving the already impressive edifice a theatrical effect. I caught a few pages in my hands: letters to the Security Council on UN stationery and reports on the situation in Cyprus, all in Arabic.

On First Avenue at 50th, a Slavic-looking man leaned on a wall, pissing right into the intersection— likely a diplomat from the nearby Slovakia or Ukraine missions. Diplomats flaunting their immunity is a common New York complaint, whether it's the Haitian ambassador's skinhead son terrorizing the eighties hardcore scene, or fires raging while hydrants are blocked by cars with diplomatic plates.

But while I mused, three police swooped in and swept the Slav up against the wall, unbuttoned pants and all. A diplomat he was not, apparently. The worst part was that I, too, needed to piss. Around the corner, the secluded side of the Singapore mission offered an opportunity, though also a risk of being caned for my crime, since—with sovereign territory—the laws of their land apply, not mine.

By the time I was finishing up in Midtown it was already 2:30 a.m. The streets were empty and the lights out. Not even stragglers or drunks to interrogate, so I resorted to other means of gathering information: the garbage. The trash at Zimbabwe's mission on 56th was a fount of information, featuring a fax from Burkina-Faso, an invitation to celebrate South Africa's Freedom Day, a coffee-stained copy of *Third World Economics*, and a discarded $10 "Simply Africa" phone card.

Contrast that with what I later found in the bags outside Angola—a $14,000 phone bill. A lot you can tell from a phone bill, too. I was confused by all the calls to Brazil until I checked the atlas and found that Brazil has the largest Portuguese-speaking population in the world. Mozambique and Angola are next, with Portugal only coming in fourth.

The Angolans' other out-of-country calls were more puzzling: Slovakia, Jamaica, Mali, and a one-night volley of 2:00 a.m. calls to France. Half of the fourteen grand was overdue charges. But I'm one to talk.

Colombia, Somalia, Pakistan—it was nice to see some flags up besides the stars and stripes, which are hard to get excited about. Fatigue was setting in, but on 65th I perked up a bit. A jewel in the crown of UN missions: Palestine. Before checking the paperwork, I'd wondered if this spot was unique in the world, perhaps the Palestinians' only sovereign territory, but I was completely off the mark. Turns out Palestine has fully recognized embassies in Albania and Algeria, a delegation in Australia, a permanent mission in Austria … you get the idea. Still, it was heartening to see one little piece of Palestinian territory not under the gun. The solitary, droopy policeman out front hardly counted.

I stopped in a bodega and got a bagel and a beer. I was on my last legs. Mechanically placing one foot in front of the next, I trudged wearily past Poland and arrived at the Russian Federation compound, which former Soviet republics Belarus and Tajikistan also occupy. One can't help but wonder what it was like in the Cold War days. My old school textbooks with their color-coded Red Scare maps never mentioned that the USSR had already taken over an entire city block on the Upper East Side.

I gazed with wonder, already half asleep and starring in some espionage thriller dream. When the clock struck 3:00, I woke with a start. Shift change at the precinct across the street. Too many cops. I beat a hasty retreat.

79th was the last stop on this worldwide, whirlwind tour. Iraq's mission lies right around the corner from the Met. Who knew? And nearby, the bright red building covered in locksmith stickers and menus for Afghani restaurants? Albania. But oh-so-very NYC.

There was but one more mission to visit in Manhattan—Bulgaria's—but I would have rather shot myself than crawled another five blocks. Besides, the satisfying sense of completion (always important for us borderline obsessive-compulsives) was impossible to achieve. Arguably, you could walk to the Central African Republic's mission in Newark, and Equatorial Guinea's in Mt. Vernon. But Kiribati, the only UN country without a US office, is hundreds of miles away from any mainland.

Fuck it! I hopped on the subway and headed home.

West Side Mole

GREETINGS, FELLOW VILLAGERS. Allow me to introduce myself. I'm the person you pass every day but don't give a moment's thought. I'm on line behind you at the post office. I'm holding the door open for you at the doctor's office. I'm admiring your dog in Abingdon Square.

We've shared the same sidewalks for years, yet you've never registered my presence except as an obstacle to maneuver around. To you, I'm on the periphery. A passing shadow, not part of the local color.

I'm unfamiliar, which is always threatening to a villager, especially in this capital-*V* Village where refusal to change is a badge of pride. I'm tolerated just as long as I keep moving and don't ask for anything— especially to be counted as an authentic part of the neighborhood I've been in for years.

In a sense my invisibility is a success, because blending in is how people like me survive. The less we stick out, the better. If we dress down and mind our own business, the landlords, lecherous creeps, and police won't ask our names and where we live. Our presence depends on our ability to remain unnoticed, like criminals in a witness protection plan.

Call me the Mole. The name fits snugly, for not only do I sleep in a hidden, homemade hole, but I also carry on a cloak-and-dagger double life. My coworkers wouldn't guess that I have no lease or legal residence, and that my existence hinges on a game of hide-and-seek.

Like most locals, we eat out when we meet. Years pass without ever seeing each other's apartments, which is perfect, since they might be alarmed that I lack a stove, fridge, window, and proper bed.

Strangers are the only ones who can see through my disguise, kindred spirits who are also on the margins. They wink knowingly when our paths cross. We recognize each other the way ex-cons—or the very rich—can pick each other out in a crowd.

There are many of us in the neighborhood, though we aren't counted in the census or mentioned by the tourist guides. We are not the official face of the Village. More like its backside.

But the moles are manifold here, even if unseen. In fact, we may be the majority. Start the tally with illegal subletters like me, then add the dogsitters and working girls. The au pairs and building supers. The cashiers and cooks who catch a few hours of sleep in the back of the shop after their double shifts. The personal assistants and art handlers who nestle in between stretchers in the galleries at night.

And the children—the neighborhood kids who grew up here but didn't think to get on the waiting list for Westbeth or the West Village Houses until it was too late. After the layoff and divorce, there was nowhere to go but mom and dad's couch.

Don't forget the people living on the street or in cars, many of whom pass as "normal," sleeping in their suits, with cell phones for alarm clocks.

Even the moles whose holes are in a different part of the city spend more time in the Village than its official, storied residents, who are always visiting their cabins upstate and summering on the Cape.

We do the degrading work that keeps the Village running while the aboveground residents write, paint, or—let's face it—sit around and complain, talking about how persecuted they are, prophesizing doom as the barbarians from above 14th Street gather at the gates.

And therein lies the real trouble. Because it's one thing to be here on a borrowed dime, doing the Village's dirty work and being overlooked and ignored. It's another to get the brunt of the scorn the neighborhood turns toward those from the outside.

To walk down my own street and be treated as an interloper and sightseer is a drag. Insult is added to injury when the local loudmouths lecture me about how antiestablishment they are. Even reading the neighborhood paper I feel vilified, because anyone under retirement age is lumped into a faceless horde. Anyone who hasn't been here since the sixties is assumed to be rich, and a fool besides.

It's enough to ruffle your fur.

Who will speak for the outsiders among the

outsiders on these lovely cobbled streets? Stay tuned for future columns as I present the Village from my hole.

2

Greetings, fellow Villagers, and a big thanks to the readers who responded to my last column, even if positive feedback might've been preferable. Luckily I am used to being called names, which is why I've acquired more than one.

An anonymous letter writer suggested I move to Bushwick—a destination akin to Ohio on the neighborhood map, which doesn't go beyond Mercer, like the delivery guys at Imperial Vintner. Another nominated me as the ideal candidate for the "home care, home share" program this paper has been trumpeting as an answer to the neighborhood's woes.

It's a stunning plan, indeed—stunning for its sense of entitlement. Simply take your average arty-but-ailing Village elder and match him with an NYU freshman, a demographic no self-respecting local would give the time of day. In exchange for living in the senior's rent-stabilized closet, the student acts as their full-time maid and health-care aid.

Failed painters and authors—failures at everything besides renting an apartment and literally going nowhere since—get waited on hand and foot by college students already struggling with a full caseload of courses. The lucky kids get to be honorary Villagers, apprenticing by wiping the asses of the cultural elite. A more insulting equation would be hard to imagine. Never mind that the poor kids have their own seniors to take care of, or will soon enough.

The other moles of the neighborhood have a name for the local landed gentry who haven't made a new painting or screenplay this century: real estate artists. Their masterpiece? The John Hancock they drew back in '67 when they signed their lease.

Don't get me wrong: me and the other moles *like* you guys, and hope to join you someday sipping lactaid lattes in the park. The whole world should live like Villagers do, with more time spent on creative pursuits than fretting about getting by. If the wealth in this country was properly distributed, and the rent control laws expanded, we could. As it stands, the sun is down and the waterfront gated long before we get off work.

It's not just jealousy that gets under my skin, it's the way that pedigree Villagers expect to have it both ways. They tout themselves as the last of the avant-garde—keepers of the flame—while keeping out those who would follow in their steps. They complain about the influx of the super rich, yet then fawn, like the editor of this paper, over celebrities who've recently arrived. They see themselves as royalty, elevated from the rabble, yet they play the victim card, crying wolf about encroaching development and reckless delivery guys on bikes.

I'll tell you this much: *I* didn't order out. You'll find me at Integral Yoga at 6:00 when the questionable leftovers get marked down, and at Lifethyme at 10:00 with the half-off steam tray crowd. In the Village, that's how the other half lives.

My purpose, however, is not to exaggerate our differences or draw lines in the sand. We all love this neighborhood we share. My point is simple: look around for the moles in your midst, and count us in. We are Villagers too.

Sadly, the editor has informed me that this column will be my last, ostensibly due to lack of space.

Restaurant Reviews

I WENT TO the diner and sat down in a booth in the back. When the waiter came, he stared at me stonily. "Who told you to sit here?" he asked. "This is a restaurant, not the city dump. This is a family business, not for crazy people and bums."

"Coffee and a scoop of ice cream." I told him. "Vanilla."

He made a sour face. "Today, no vanilla."

He shook his head then smacked his lips in disgust and walked away. I leaned back and read the paper. I waited a few minutes for my coffee before realizing it was right in front of me, placed there silently, expertly.

I took a sip. It burned, but nicely. Then the bell on the door rang. I turned to look, expecting Skip, but it was the professor instead. He shuffled into a seat two booths down from me, as always. He made little nesting noises, unpacking his bags slowly, methodically.

Besides the two of us, the place was almost empty. A deaf couple signed to each other at a table by the window. An older guy sat at the counter eating soup. A steady trickle of strippers, cab drivers, and cops came and went, but they were all orders to go, no one we would be getting to know.

The professor tucked himself into a book, covered his ears with a massive pair of headphones, and immersed himself in his true love. He sat there as he did every night, a stack of language tapes on the table, devouring them one by one.

The diner was silent, no music to drown out your thoughts. Like the professor, the regulars here came to work and think things over in peace. They kept to themselves for the most part. They chose their words carefully.

"What's the matter, you don't like my coffee?" The waiter was looking down on me with sad, serious eyes. Old world eyes. Albanian, he was, I knew from many overheard conversations, something that couldn't be helped here. I'd even ventured to discuss with him Ismail Kadare, the Albanian author. But now I was at a loss for words, pinned down by his gaze.

"No," I stammered, shrinking under the scrutiny. "I love your coffee."

"This is love?" He pointed at my half-empty cup, growing cold. He hung his head, hurt.

I cast my eyes down in shame. When I got the courage to lift them again, a fresh, steaming cup was there in his place.

The beautiful, birdlike movements of the deaf couple's hands kept me hypnotized, fluttering in the corner of my eyes. I kicked myself, tried to look instead out the window at shapes of people passing by, but even that felt invasive. I looked at the clock. Where the hell was Skip? I was getting impatient.

He must be lost, I figured. He's never been here

before, and my directions weren't the best. Might as well catch up on my mail while I wait.

I took out a pad of paper and started a letter. For the date, I put down Christmas Day. "It'll seem more desperate that way," whispered a little voice in my ear. "You know, grittier, more urgent. Trust me." It was the coffee talking—or Ian, who sounded uncannily like my main complex, a persecution-and-messiah mix.

Truth be told, it was Chanukah, the sixth night, and I'd spent the whole week traipsing from one lovely Jewish lady to the next, kindling the candles, singing the prayers, and most important, eating the delicious homemade latkes. No wonder I wasn't hungry now.

A lifetime of being the only Jew for miles, and now I was making up for lost time among a million. But to believe the letter I was writing I was hungry, cold, and dying of loneliness. Ian's voice, gaining the upper hand in my head, dictated the whole thing. As could be expected, it was full of lies and wild exaggerations, and barely legible.

I ripped it up, placing the pieces in a neat stack next to the cream and sugar. I laughed a little under my breath. Used to think my letters would be published, now they're not even sent. Well, that's life.

I looked over at the professor to check how he was doing. I leaned forward as far as possible to peek over his shoulder and see what he was studying, but the tapes were cradled by his side like a baby, out of my view. That's what I should be doing, I knew: something productive, something real. Look at the professor—so smart he was, yet *he* didn't lecture. Just once in a while he'd take off the headphones and catch someone off guard. "Excuse me," he'd say. "I couldn't help overhearing you mention that your wife is from Vanuatu, is that correct? Please tell her 'Xxbxgl wwb xxxf' from me. Good day."

That was cool. That was how I wanted to be. Or like the waiter, firm but sweet.

I picked at my teeth with a fingernail. I looked at the reflection in the napkin dispenser: pale, except for dark bags under the eyes. I growled at the image, which didn't help.

Skip, I thought. Skip, where are you? If there's one thing I hate, it's being stood up. It's starting to feel like Christmas Day for real, and that's not good.

Skip, I really hope you didn't get into a horrible accident on the way. If there's a message on the machine saying you're dead when I get home, I'm going to feel awful about being mad at you now. There are so many things we have yet to say and do together. But if you're not dead and didn't call, I'm going to kill you.

Up at the counter, the soup guy started on a little soliloquy, a curtain call before going out into the cold, made all the more dramatic by his voice revving up suddenly after a long silence. It rattled and rumbled like a kettledrum, then took flight like a clarinet. What a voice! Smoke a pack a day and gargle with glass, you still wouldn't sound like that; not without a lifetime of experience to give it character and shape. He faced the waiter but spoke to no one in particular—and at the same time, to everyone in the room. I turned to watch.

"Cold? You call this cold?" He was talking about the weather, but the way he spoke gave you a warm, happy feeling inside. He laughed, staccato like a machine gun. "You go back to the forties and fifties, now *that* was cold. Brrr! Middle of December like this, you're not out on a pleasant stroll in the park. Nuh-uh. Cuz it's *zero*, man. It's not just a little breeze. You want to make it around the corner, you'd best get yourself a snowplow. Back then it was really something. Talk about cold. Ha! We got some *beautiful* weather now."

He let out a little spiral of steam, whistling at the wonder of it all. Then he put on his coat and strolled out the door. "Alright, then," he said, and it was. But in the second it took for the door to close, an arctic wind tore through the place, causing everyone to shudder.

"The forties and fifties?" I thought. "That's ridiculous. Impossible. That guy would have to be seventy, at least. Well, maybe so. Seniors are pretty sprightly in New York. You're not old until eighty-five."

"More coffee for you, my friend?" It was the waiter, a very persistent man.

"Sure," I nodded, trying to hold onto the thread of my thoughts with one hand. How much coffee did they drink in Albania? This was obscene.

I wondered, could it really have been that much colder in a different era? That was crazy. It must've just seemed that way.

But my thoughts were interrupted once again. "Sit somewhere else," the waiter was curtly telling someone. "Don't bother him."

I looked up, surprised to find that my booth was the one in question. In a world of waiters angling to kick me out, here was one ready to defend my honor to loiter and linger. My heart swelled with gratitude. Still, I waved him away. "This time," I said grandly, "it's okay."

He took a step back but continued to cast a suspicious glare as Skip slipped past him into my booth and reached across the table to give me a half-hug. "I'm really sorry I'm late," he said. "I tried to look it up, but you never told me the name of this place."

I smiled, overcome with a boyish glee just to be in the presence of an old pal. A nostalgic glow swept over us both. Once reserved for the distant past, it seemed to be making its way into my present life an awful lot.

"The movie started forty minutes late," Skip explained. "The film collector who owns the print couldn't find a parking place, so while he drove around, everyone had to wait."

"That sucks," I said.

"Actually, it was really entertaining because every one of the four people there—the four paying customers—was a *Fangoria*-reading, convention-going, gay horror fan from New Jersey, and while we waited, they were arguing in the lobby in the snobbiest, nerdiest tones, with the most elite attitudes, about the schlockiest, crappiest horror movies. I brought up *Maniac Cop 1* and *2* and they looked at me like I'd taken a dump on the table. They were aghast, like, 'Exactly *what* did you find so likable about *Maniac Cop 1* and *2*?'"

The waiter came and hovered over us. He stood

there, arms folded. He tapped his foot, he sucked his teeth. Skip stopped cold.

"Are you going to keep me waiting forever? I am a busy man. Do you expect me to wait all night for you to decide what kind of ice cream you want?"

"Chocolate!" I called out quickly, like on a quiz show, relieved to be let off so easily.

"You want chocolate, I bring you chocolate. Fine. Why didn't you say so in the first place? Also something for your friend to eat instead of running at the mouth."

A moment later, a plate of fries was set down along with the ice cream. Before Skip could order, the waiter turned his back. "Professor!" he yelled, wanting to be heard over the headphones as he headed that way. "Professor, you are a very naive man. That's what you are, naive."

The professor didn't seem to mind the intrusion. Tittering and clucking, he pulled off his headset. "Yes, well, I suppose so," he said fondly, warming up to the waiter who now stood idling by his side in a state of attention. "It's true, I'm a very trusting person. Incidentally, do you know how to say 'ice cream' in the language they are speaking?" He pointed his chin very quietly toward the window.

"Like so."

A Visit with John Holmstrom

I'D ADMIRED John Holmstrom's work since I was a wee lad, and had a long list of questions I was dying to ask. He was amenable to the idea and agreed to meet me at a nearby diner—the same one that held the fateful conference where Henry joined Black Flag.

I was hopeful this meeting would have a happier outcome, but a party of Ukrainians sat down at the next table for a post-wedding celebration just as we began to chat. As a result, my recording serves as a better record of their conversation than ours. And so, with what direct quotes I can salvage, the story will proceed in my own words.

Holmstrom came to New York City from Connecticut in 1972 to learn to draw comics. He enrolled at the School for Visual Arts, but was disappointed to find not a single cartooning class. Along with some other angry students, he went to the president of the school. "Sure, what cartoonists do you want?" they were asked. "Put a list together."

And so they did—a fantasy list of comics legends. Topping the list was Will Eisner (the maverick who'd created the Spirit in 1940, and, famously, turned down publishing the first issue of *Superman*) and Harvey Kurtzman (the founder of the original *Mad* magazine). The administration surprised the students by hiring both.

Studying under Eisner and Kurtzman was Holmstrom's first entry into the worlds of comics and publishing. Their lessons, and their belief in him, greatly affected the course of his life. Even after he could no longer afford the steep SVA tuition and was forced to drop out, Holmstrom continued as their apprentice, literally as well as figuratively: both Eisner and Kurtzman hired him as personal assistant. The work was part-time and only paid minimum wage, but that was all he needed to scrape by. More importantly, it gave the young artist an opportunity to hone his own skills.

Holmstrom's first published work was *Domeland*, an educational comic book put out by Charas—later to become a Puerto Rican activist organization with a massive squat on Avenue B, but at the time a less political group operating out of an acre-wide lot on Cherry Street where they built geodesic domes.

To Charas, these structures were the perfect shelter: indestructible, aerodynamic, affordable, and environmentally sound. Charas (and *Domeland*) promoted them as an answer to the world's housing woes—and they were all set to go to India to demonstrate, with Holmstrom in tow. Then someone from the Indian government looked up the group's name in a Spanish-English dictionary, and the deal was off.

Instead, the domes were built in the South Bronx, where it took resourceful youth only two or three days to blow them up.

Holmstrom was embarrassed by *Domeland*, as anyone should be of their earliest work, and he neglected to keep even one copy. His next output, a cover illustration for *Screw* (of a woman putting ketchup on a severed penis in a hotdog bun) embarrassed everyone else.

Kurtzman, who'd landed Holmstrom the *Screw* cover, then angled him into a freelance job at Scholastic, drawing a monthly strip for *Bananas*, their magazine for seventh and eighth graders. "It was a great gig," Holmstrom remembers. "Three hundred dollars per strip, and back then, you could get an apartment in New York for a hundred dollars a month."

What happened next was a happy accident. Kurtzman had lined him up with yet another job, this one as editor of an ambitiously large, soon-to-be-launched humor magazine called *National Harpoon*, a *National Lampoon* spoof. Holmstrom was hired, only to find out that *Harpoon*'s backers had no intention of actually publishing. Their plan was to get bought out by *National Lampoon* before even getting off the ground.

That disappointment turned into inspiration, setting off bells in Holmstrom's head. "It started getting into my mind what I could do with a national magazine," he says.

Helping Kurtzman had never been a steady job, and Will Eisner closed his office every summer, so

Holmstrom was cut off from day-to-day work. He was restless. He ran into Eddie McNiel, an old friend from high school with whom he'd once founded a comedy group. McNiel had stuck with the troupe while Holmstrom pursued other avenues, but now he was sick of it. He was restless, too.

McNiel invited Holmstrom to return to their hometown for the summer to work for a painting business started by another old friend, Ged. Once reunited in Connecticut, the three men got along so well that Ged suggested they pool their energies and form a company—for publishing instead of painting.

And so it was that in the summer of '75, in Ged's downtown Cheshire apartment, *Punk* (and perhaps punk itself) was born.

As summer came to an end, Holmstrom returned to Eisner's office. McNiel—henceforth known by his nickname, Legs—was making porno flicks at Total Impact, a hippie film cooperative at Second Avenue and 14th, sharing the office with such future film luminaries as Victor Colicchio (*Summer of Sam*) and Mary Harron (*I Shot Andy Warhol, American Psycho*). Movie buffs may or may not want to seek out the one film all three worked on together: a porno called *Blow Dry*.

Ged went back to school to finish his degree, but called just a few months later: "Ah, I'm bored in school, I hate it here. Let's start the company now."

Great!

Holmstrom went to find their new venture some office space, but nothing seemed right or within their price range. Having already given thirty-day notice on his apartment, and with the date drawing close, Holmstrom was nervous. Then a real estate agent brought him to the no-man's-land tucked between Hell's Kitchen, the rail yards, and the entrance to the Lincoln Tunnel. Abandoned train tracks ran overhead; rats the size of cats lurked on the docks down the block.

The building for rent—a huge storefront, with a complete office setup already in place—was eerily abandoned, as if the previous tenants had disappeared into thin air. Sweaters still hung on the backs of chairs, half-full coffee cups rested on the desks.

"We can get rid of all this junk," the realtor said.

"No, no—it's perfect!" said Holmstrom. "We'll take it." He and Legs came up with the two hundred bucks needed to secure the place, and Ged arrived a couple weeks later.

The Dictators were chosen for the cover of their debut issue, but a quick call to Epic Records brought news that the band had just broken up.

"Let's go see the Ramones and do a story on them," Holmstrom suggested. With a reel-to-reel recorder and someone from Total Impact along to take pictures, they headed to CBGB's on the Sunday after Thanksgiving.

After interviewing the Ramones, it turned out that Lou Reed was in the audience, and he reluctantly agreed to talk to them too, resulting in one of the most incisive and hilarious interviews ever published.

The whole magazine came together fast—so fast that they wrote the wrong year on the copyright page.

A bit of paste-up and it was delivered to the printer (the same guy who'd done *Domeland*) on Christmas. On New Year's Eve Holmstrom stopped by to check on the progress, and finding the printer hard at work, rolled up his sleeves to help.

On January 1st, 1976, *Punk* #1 hit the streets. CB's was only two blocks from the printer, so Legs and Holmstrom were able to deliver their baby right into waiting hands.

Punk stood out immediately from other magazines of the period. Visually it was striking, with bold graphics, bawdy cartoons, and photo-comic narratives inspired by the French "photo funnies" from the forties that Kurtzman had brought into class.

Holmstrom employed a "less is more" attitude, expressing his ideas with very few words. In part, he credits minimalism. "Musicians weren't hanging around art galleries, but everyone was aware of the artistic scene in New York at the time, and the better bands were trying to present a new visual form as well as a new musical form. I wanted *Punk* to be like that, too."

Punk covered the culture of rock 'n' roll, and did so with a swaggering, take-no-prisoners attitude. It was intentionally shocking, the way rock 'n' roll had once been, back when DJs smashed records on the air and Senate subcommittees linked comic books and rock 'n' roll to juvenile delinquency.

Holmstrom wanted to bring back that connection and run with it—not just the shocking energy, but the coupling of rock 'n' roll with comics, two art forms that had grown up side by side. "We wanted to be the *Mad* magazine of rock 'n' roll," he says.

So, the new rag that rang in the Bicentennial was a synthesis of many sources: forties film mags, fifties rock 'n' roll, and sixties underground press; comic books (both underground and mainstream) and the original, Kurtzman-produced *Mad* magazine; the shittyness and grittiness of New York in the seventies, and art school ideas about minimalism.

But what really set *Punk* apart—what made it not just a groundbreaking magazine, but the spark that lit the fire which remains so close to our hearts—was something else.

In large part, it was Legs's fault. He had always wanted to be a PR guy. "Look," he said, "if you want an idea to be successful, you've got to make it bigger than the magazine. We're gonna start a punk *movement.*"

He took a very small scene in a Hells Angels hangout on the Bowery and cast it larger than life. "I'm gonna be a punk," Legs declared, assuming the role of pinup boy and archetype for the new movement, one that's changed very little in all the years since.

Of course it was laughable, not to mention megalomaniacal, but it worked. In New York anyone could go down to CBGB's, see that this "movement" consisted of three or four bands and a handful of their friends, and dismiss it outright. Not so in England, where through distributors *Punk* reached readers who took Legs's fantasy seriously. Blondie returned from their first European tour with reports of London kids dressed up like Legs, acting out scenes from the pages of *Punk* #1, and calling themselves punks.

They took to it completely. Only one thing missing: the music. In January of 1976 there were no punk records in existence. The Ramones first UK tour, famous for supposedly launching British punk, was still six months away. According to Rat Scabies of the Damned, the London kids formed their own bands by looking at the pictures from the pages of *Punk* and trying to guess what the music sounded like. Even when they got it wrong, they got it right.

The release of the Ramones debut LP also came about partly as a result of the first issue of *Punk*. "We got them their first record contract," Holmstrom claims. "Our initial story on the Ramones convinced Seymour Stein from Sire Records that he had to sign them and make them the first hit out of CBGB's." The iconic cover image came from a *Punk* photo shoot, snapped by CB's doorwoman Roberta Bayley in one of her first ever attempts to use a camera.

The exact location of the photograph remains a mystery. Legs and Arturo Vega (Ramones' art director) maintain it was taken at the community garden on 2nd Street between First and Second Avenues. Holmstrom remembers it happening elsewhere, but as to where he hasn't a clue, and Bayley herself has forgotten too. (The photo on the third album was shot in the alley behind CBGB's—that much we know for sure.)

Punk #1 was an instant hit by all accounts. Subscription requests started coming in after just a few days. The *Village Voice* called *Punk* "the zeitgeist of a new generation."

"That was our peak," Holmstrom sighs. "From there, it goes downhill. Everything falls apart."

The problem was a matter of perspective: what seemed like a success to *Punk* readers was a complete failure in the eyes of its creators, whose expectations were much, much higher. They'd expected to get rich, or at least make a decent living, from their efforts. Instead, months passed and Holmstrom, Legs, and Ged were still sharing living as well as working quarters at the Tenth Avenue storefront—now known as the Punk Dump—and struggling to get the mag out monthly and keep up with the bills.

Add to this the age-old problems of publishing: distributors that don't pay, printers that are chronically late, advertisers who abandon ship if the magazine fails to come out on time. It was hard to reconcile the fact that *Punk* was getting tons of press and the magazine was an international sensation, yet it only seemed to get more difficult to produce instead of less.

Their visions of grandeur were perhaps unrealistic, but not unprecedented. After all, punk rock seemed poised to be the Next Big Thing, and they were on the crest of the wave.

Holmstrom explains: "I thought the Ramones would be bigger than the Beatles. I'd seen the examples of, say, Alice Cooper, who went from being the most hated, reviled rock band in LA to number one with a bullet. That seemed to be the formula for success in rock 'n' roll. Everybody hated Jimi Hendrix when he first came out. He was kicked off the Monkees tour by the Daughters of the American Revolution. Then he became the biggest star in the universe.

"People hated the Beatles when they came out, they hated the Rolling Stones. Everything in rock 'n' roll had this rebellious spirit that people tried to stop. So I figured, 'Hey, they hate it! We're gonna be rich! We're right where we want to be.'

"Because, really, we were just following the formula for success. Only, ironically, when it came to punk, the formula stopped working."

The bottom line was, they were broke. Despite daydreams of fame and fortune, the real goal was just to make enough to eat. Luckily, Holmstrom still had his freelance work for *Bananas* and other magazines on the side, and that provided enough for him to get by.

In hindsight, he realizes that *Punk* should have been subsidized by his freelance work and kept going no matter what. But, in the summer of '76, things seemed bleak. Issue #5 was abysmal, shunned by readers and staff alike. With little remaining resources or hope, they decided to call it quits.

And that would have been the end of our tale, if not for the entrance of an unexpected visitor. Holmstrom was sitting around the Dump dejectedly when a man walked in and kicked his feet up on the desk. "I'm gonna make you rich and famous," he said, punctuating his claim with a crisp hundred-dollar bill for each of the *Punk* staff. With that, he bid farewell: "I'll be in touch."

The man was Tom Forcade, already a legend in underground publishing, though our bewildered boys didn't know that yet.

Forcade's life deserves an article of its own, if not a full book. His abbreviated CV begins in the sixties as a small-time Arizona drug dealer who learned to fly, making his own trips over the border to Mexico and Colombia as a way to cut out the middleman. Soon he'd made a small fortune. Publishing an underground magazine, *Orpheum*, led to involvement with the Underground Press Syndicate, a half-dozen papers with an agreement to freely reprint each other's work.

Under Forcade's stewardship, and thanks to his organizational skills, it grew into a powerhouse with two hundred members worldwide. Next, he engineered a deal with microfilm company Bell & Howell to preserve for posterity all the sixties papers, big and small, while providing them with funds to persevere for another few years.

Called in front of a Senate subcommittee investigating pornography, he introduced the pie toss as a form of political protest. Angry at corporate control of rock music, he founded the Rock Liberation Front, going up against Warner Brothers for their attempted takeover of Woodstock, and confronting Phil Spector for pocketing the proceeds from the benefit album for Bangladesh.

Forcade was everywhere at once, including the 1972 Republican convention, where police—finding smoke bombs in his van—accused him of a plot to assassinate Richard Nixon.

He was forced to go on the lam—and that's when another epiphany hit: Why not start a magazine to bring underground culture to the mainstream?

A year later his idea was a reality, and the magazine, *High Times*, was selling a million copies a month. Two years after that, he walked into *Punk*.

Forcade was a miracle, exactly what Holmstrom & co. desperately needed: a benefactor to bring their dream back to life—one with unparalleled experience in distribution and publishing. It seemed a perfect fit.

Punk #6 followed, published under the auspices of *High Times*. It was their first full-length photo comic, a film on paper called *The Legend of Nick Detroit*, with Richard Hell playing the lead role and David Johansen, Debbie Harry, and the Talking Heads, among others, in support.

The all-star cast was as much of an accident as the photo comics Kurtzman had done in the early sixties featuring Gloria Steinem, Terry Gilliam and John Cleese (both later of Monty Python), R. Crumb, and even Woody Allen. For Kurtzman, like Holmstrom fifteen years later, those were just the people hanging around his office at the time.

Nick Detroit was an innovative, exciting experiment—and a complete flop. Forcade unceremoniously dropped *Punk* like a hot rock, though later he would be back. For now it was back to square one.

Holmstrom's history is full of such false starts and just plain bad luck, but also a surprising amount of eleventh-hour saves. Once again, a mysterious investor appeared, this one from Detroit, drawn in by all the *Nick Detroit* posters plastered around town. He dropped twenty grand into the coffers of the nearly moribund mag, and soon the presses were rolling again, with some of *Punk*'s best issues to date.

Issue #8 featured a cover story on the Sex Pistols at a time when few in America had heard of the band. Unlike Legs, who considered the London scene a pale imitation, Holmstrom was thrilled by the new energy.

"They improved on our formula," he says. "When I first heard the Sex Pistols record, I was blown away. No, I was never competitive about it. That was Legs's thing. He didn't have an understanding that it would be good if punk rock happened in another city and in another way."

Similarly, Holmstrom was supportive of the fanzines that followed in *Punk*'s footsteps ("Just as long as they didn't think they were better than us"). The first issue of *Sniffin' Glue* arrived in the mail in the summer of '76 with a fan letter from editor Mark P. "Then all of a sudden," says Holmstrom, "the third issue, there's a shift. Then I'm getting letters like, 'Oh, you Americans, you're rich, and you suck. We live on the dole. You don't know what suffering is.' What a load of shit!"

Still, he acknowledges *Sniffin' Glue*'s awesomeness (and, in truth, it *was* even better than *Punk*) but prefers its lesser-remembered UK contemporary, *Ripped & Torn*. The flood of English zines was made possible by Rough Trade, who took the profits from importing copies of *Punk* and bought a mimeograph machine for all the kids to use to make their own. "They didn't need us anymore," laments *Punk*'s editor, sounding both proud and sad.

As for Legs, his involvement in *Punk*—though crucial at its inception—was actually rather limited, according to Holmstrom: "He contributed a little bit to the first issue, then took off with the second issue. Then he and Ged had a big falling out, had a fistfight on the floor trying to kill each other, and he was kicked out."

Legs returned, but borrowed Ged's bed—and a bottle of maple syrup—for a threesome. That was the last straw.

Two cofounders were left, and soon they were embroiled in a conflict of their own. *Punk* #9 was all set to go to press—in Holmstrom's opinion, the best one yet, featuring the Damned, a comic interview of Kiss, and advance excerpts of William S. Burroughs's *Junkie*—when Ged announced that this issue would have to be their last.

There was no money left. The twenty grand was already gone, pissed away on bad business decisions and the fancy, glossy paper that Ged had picked. The rest of the staff was justifiably pissed. "It was like the Julius Caesar assassination," says Holmstrom. "We ended up firing him right before it was going to come back from the printer."

Ged decided to get revenge. He went to the printer and told them *Punk* didn't have enough in the bank to pay the bill, which turned out to be true. Holmstrom had to personally borrow money to get *Punk* out of hock. Then the printer, finally paid in full, went belly-up. Holmstrom never did get the magazines back, nor the cash—not even the originals, which included one-of-a-kind polaroids of Burroughs and Ginsberg in Mexico hanging out on the beach.

Not only was it a disaster in every respect, but *Punk* was now in debt. Someone suggested a benefit, and a whole weekend of shows at CB's was quickly set up. Blondie, the Dead Boys, the Cramps, and Patti Smith all played. The Dictators' Ross the Boss jumped onstage to jam, as did Fred Smith, who had left Blondie to join Television, confident that they would be the more successful band.

That was when the paradigm at CB's was undergoing a radical shift: Blondie and the Ramones—both of whom had been considered a joke—were becoming hugely popular, while the more polished, groomed-for-success groups were left in the dust. Blondie's contract on the small Private Stock label was bought out by Chrysalis. The Ramones' label, Sire—then still a small independent—was scooped up by Warner Brothers.

Punk Rock was now a big business; *Punk* magazine was still a total bust. As always, the musical aspects of the scene received support and acclaim while the print media that formed its cultural underpinnings and helped promote the bands ate shit.

That set the tone for what was to come, three decades of great fanzines morphing into mostly mediocre record labels (Slash, Touch & Go, Sub Pop, Lookout, No Idea) and fanzine editors who achieved renown only through their later bands (Kevin Seconds, Thurston Moore, King Vitamin of the Butthole Surfers, Dave Grubbs of Slint).

Anyone who's done both a fanzine and a band knows that playing music is always more rewarding, and—kill me for saying so, but it's true—less work.

At any rate, Holmstrom was back in the black after the benefit, and back at the grind, but the issues that followed were lacking a little spunk. Someone had taken the piss out of *Punk*. The magazine mirrored what the Ramones were going through at the time—a process of streamlining paired with increased production values and a nod to the mainstream.

Rocket to Russia and *Road to Ruin* were certainly great albums (and drawing the art for both earned Holmstrom enough to get his own apartment and move out of the Dump). So were the corresponding issues of *Punk*. But getting back to basics meant becoming a bit tame and formulaic. Full-color photos came next, helping neither the band nor mag.

To further the analogy, it wasn't until *Too Tough to Die* that the Ramones reconnected with the spirit that had made them so special, and they did so not by paring down but by branching out, surprising everyone by incorporating hardcore into their trademark sound— in essence, picking fruit from the tree they'd planted.

Punk's version of *Too Tough to Die* was *Mutant Monster Beach Party*, a full-length photo comic starring Joey Ramone, and it also came after a period of stumbling in the wilderness. *Mutant Monster Beach*

Party was a true masterpiece, an amazing mix of music, photos, comic illustration, and a deranged plot about juvenile delinquents—a climax of all the disparate elements of *Punk* coming together in perfect harmony.

The issue was another total loss, but if you measure success by sales alone, sticking to a predictable formula is best.

In the meantime, Forcade had reentered the picture. Not only did he agree to go back to publishing *Punk*, he enlisted Holmstrom for a pet project of his own: an underground movie documenting the upcoming Sex Pistols US tour.

Forcade had grandiose ideas about the movie—sure to gross a million bucks—and the accompanying book that Holmstrom would produce (plus a special edition of *Punk*). Most of all, he wanted to get back at his old nemesis Warner Brothers, the corporate profiteer, who was running the tour.

They set off with a crew to film the band as they wound their way through the entrails of America, leaving a path of destruction in their wake. But things with the film did not go as Forcade had foreseen. Warner Brothers remembered him all too well and wanted nothing to do with the pie-throwing, Phil Spector-confronting madman. They did everything in their power to prevent his movie from being made.

Meanwhile, back at home, Forcade's staff was in revolt, afraid that *High Times* would go bankrupt from the hundreds of thousands of dollars being drained from its account on some ridiculous escapade. The

Pistols themselves were of course a total mess, finally self-destructing in San Francisco like everyone else. As Holmstrom arrived back in New York, so did Johnny and Sid, the latter dopesick and headed for the hospital, the former crashing out on someone's floor, without enough money to make it the rest of the way home.

What a hell of a week and a half!

Forcade's movie, *D.O.A.*, turned out to be yet another casualty of that tour—it took three and a half years to come out. On only one count was he right: *Punk's* Sex Pistols tour journal was their best-selling issue yet.

Forcade had promised to make *Punk* as successful as *High Times*, and it might've even happened were it not for the exclusive distribution deal Forcade had signed with the notorious *Hustler* publisher, Larry Flynt. The ink was still fresh on the contract when Flynt got shot.

"When that fucker shot Flynt, he pulled the rug out from under us," Holmstrom says, shaking his head. "*High Times* started getting late payments for their distribution. The whole company was thrown into chaos.

"Oh, I've got a million of them. A million reasons why we weren't successful, and that's just one." Less laughable—and a more accurate shot—was Forcade's suicide later that year, which severed *Punk*'s lifeline once and for all.

To enumerate every failure of *Punk* would take all night, and any reader of this piece has enough of her or his own bad luck to consider. Besides, my coffee was getting cold, the waitress having cut us off after realizing we weren't going to order anything more than a side of pierogis and a grilled cheese. Mercifully, she let us stay. The place was otherwise empty now that the wedding party had left, and outside it was pissing rain.

Holmstrom's story was always ending but never over. Like the scene of the same name, *Punk* died again and again. It wasn't until 1981 that it was really down for the count. Altogether, eighteen issues had been produced, three of which never came out (lost to the inky clutches of every magazine's best friend and worst enemy, its printer).

But rather than rest—or learn his lesson— Holmstrom leapt right back into the fray with a new publication called *Comical Funnies*, a collaboration with three other cartoonists that had been involved at the tail-end of *Punk*: Bruce Carleton, Ken Weiner, and the then-unknown, fresh-faced Peter Bagge.

Holmstrom felt invigorated to work on a project completely divorced from the music industry, and he remembers the parties and collaborative energy of *Comical Funnies* fondly.

Inevitably, it couldn't last: Bagge and the others were headed towards full-length comic books while the somewhat old-fashioned newspaper editor in Holmstrom yearned for a more mixed format.

His next magazine, a free monthly called *Stop*, reflected that, with interviews of Richard Price and Soupy Sales, stunning pics by Godlis, a column by Joey Ramone, and Holmstrom reporting about "punxploitation" in Hollywood movies. At a time when other punk pioneers were writing dismissive, self-serving drivel about the new generation, he was insightful, articulate, and generous.

By 1983, *Stop* was over and the freelance jobs had dried up (Holmstrom's art for the Ramones had somewhat backfired, making his style synonymous with the band rather than leading to other work). For regular employment, he returned first to Scholastic and then to *High Times*, where the new editor knew his comics and remembered his old association with Forcade.

His first assignment: an illustrated interview with Eldridge Cleaver, which Cleaver later wrote to thank him for. Despite a few cheap shots, it was honest, which he appreciated.

Holmstrom stayed at *High Times* throughout the late eighties and all of the nineties, slowly rising up the ranks until he was publisher. In that role, he was able to bring the magazine back to its most successful peak.

Eventually the work got to be too stressful. In 2000, he left the magazine (except for the "Pot 40" list which he still writes, a spin-off from the old *Punk* and *Stop* top 40). "I'd saved up a lot of money," he says. "And I decided to try to bring back *Punk*."

The results were mixed, the response worse. Some accused him of a cynical attempt to cash in on the newfound popularity of punk rock, others of trying to relive his lost youth. Both charges contained a bit of truth. Like most reunions, the relaunch was ill-advised and a little embarrassing, but pure of heart.

At any rate, Holmstrom and the new *Punk* were subject to the same old school bad luck they'd always enjoyed. Terrorists blew up their office downtown. Distributors ripped them off. A publisher could not be found.

"I tried to do it out of my apartment," he says, "but it just about killed me. I live in a fourth-floor walk-up, so when you have to go up and down the stairs carrying boxes of magazines, it's just too much, especially at my age. Anybody can put out a little fanzine out of their apartment, but if you're gonna do ten thousand copies, you need to spend money on an office."

(I politely disagree, but happen to be blessed with a second-floor walk-up—though not the absurdly cheap rent of an apartment moved into in 1977 with a check from the Ramones as down payment. Sigh.)

And what's Holmstrom up to now? Not what you might've guessed. He's pleased as punch about a licensing deal just signed with a clothing company in Japan.

"They've brought out this crazy line of clothing," he says, gushing a bit. "It's very high-quality stuff, like '*Punk*' in glitter lettering on a very expensive women's top. Little girl pants with the anti-disco editorial from *Punk* #1 and 'John Holmstrom' printed on the inside.

"They've got coats and hoodies with the *Punk* logo on it. I'm a big brand in Japan right now. They even like some of my characters from *Domeland*. They want to make toys and action figures out of all this stuff. It's kicked my creativity in a whole new direction. I'm preparing to bring out this stuff in America, and I think it's going to sell really well."

We shall see.

With a gleam in his eye, he explains: "It's like a reward for all the crap I've put up with over the years."

The Downtown Photographers

WHAT IF LIFE was glossy like the magazines I had printed overseas, where the matte finish I ordered arrived with an inch of shellac? You could pour beer over a copy and not even get the pages wet.

Robert Frank would've showed up at my work like a father figure, as he had for filmmaker Jem Cohen—or even as a questionable mentor, as he had for several young women I knew.

"You chose this road," he would say. "It's a hard one with few rewards, but when you die they'll name it after you."

That would've warmed my heart more than, "Four dollars for a Thomas Hardy paperback? You've got to be kidding. I'll give you two."

Rather than give him the millionaire's discount, I offered a glare and a growl. A week later he was dead, but I hadn't broken my promise to keep from attacking bookstore customers.

I'd had a rule in my younger days: only drink coffee out, never at home. That pushed me to be more public, which led to adventure, or so the theory went. Now I started walking downtown only when it rained.

I used back issues as rain gear, but that didn't keep my feet from getting wet.

My friends were busy cramming for their immigration appointments. Their paper husbands and wives had paid half up front, with the remainder due when citizenship arrived. "Which side of the bed does he sleep on? What brand of toothpaste does she use?" I asked the same questions about people in the windows I passed, but didn't know the answers for my own life.

Photographers seemed to be the only people left downtown. Bob Gruen was cut from the same cloth as Frank—a grouchy prick—so I tried to fix him with the same curse. He was always in front of me at the Hudson Street post office, sending overpriced prints to overseas collectors (none taken more recently than 1978) that required proof of delivery for every package. It was like being stuck behind Lonely Planet at the all-night Oakland post office in the nineties. You'd be there till dawn, staring at the back of their Crocodile Dundee hats.

Cozy Soup & Burger served the best split pea in town. I drank it like a beverage, blistering my mouth and leaving embarrassing stains on my jeans. The world receded—only rock photographers, Cozy's staff, and me. Apparently we were the only voyeurs who still needed the public to get off.

Godlis could be seen shooting graffiti now that street life was ancient history. He seemed cool and unassuming, not that a little ego is a bad thing. Glen E. Friedman was always on 10th with his son by his side. You could tell he was a god in his kid's eyes—the ultimate litmus test, and the hardest to pass. He was in good shape, unlike most folks with a camera around their neck.

Roberta Bayley looked good, too, but she hadn't taken a picture in years. I liked to think she came out in bad weather out of solidarity with her peers. More likely her poodle had to piss.

The rain brought out invisible graffiti in the cement, like a print in a tray of developer, or lemon juice in between lines of a book heated over a match.

Two Poems

Raymond DeCapite

I found a new obscure author I love
He captures the tenderness and absurdity of life so well
Riding the train while reading his novel
my eyes flashed and got real big
Then the lids lowered conspiratorially
and got a sneaky squint
My lips curled up at the edges
like a cat that ate a bird
so pleasantly pleased

Then I realized:
Ha! I must look exactly like Yvette!

The next night I got to the part
Where the hero loses the girl
The stupid book broke my heart
and on the train home I looked like myself again
Yvette was gone

Optometrist

Jem's optometrist is Russian
Her father had the same trade
His father too

On the hallway wall
is the family heirloom
An eye exam form
for Mayakovsky

The Prevalence of Messianic Tendencies in Cross-Country Walking Guys

I GOT A CALL from a walking guy. Tzipora, AKA Zippo, had given him my number.

Later, she apologized. "He didn't seem crazy at first."

She had adopted me when I was new in town, along with Vanessa and Ruth. Together they were my advisory board—a trio of older sisters who bossed me around as if I were a hopelessly green teen from the sticks, which wasn't far from the truth.

They exaggerated our differences, including our slight difference in age. I was happy to play along, just like I'm happy to introduce Zippo as my "kid sister" now that the AARP floods our mailboxes and seniority is nothing to brag about, especially to available young men.

I count on out-of-town visitors to round out my perspective of the world now that Vanessa and Ruth are busy with kids of their own. That's why I told the walking guy I'd join him for a few miles of his epic trek from—his words—"the Golden Gate to Plymouth Rock."

We met on the West Side Highway. He was easy to spot, composed of traditional walking-guy stock:

dirty, scraggly hair and a somewhat affected air. His false humility wouldn't prevent him from accepting any award I'd brought.

Instead I asked, "Where's your pack?"

"I stashed it at my host's pad," he said. "I'm not in any hurry to move on. People are in such a rush all the time, but I guess that's typical New York."

"It's November," I pointed out.

"And?"

"Winter, man. Snow. Ice. Freezing to death on the side of the road if you don't get to the finish line fast."

"Good point," he brightened up. "Maybe I'll wait till spring to head to Connecticut."

Oy vey. A *fake* walking guy, on his epic journey from the couch to the fridge at some poor fool's pad. I'd met his type before. In fact, I'd been his type for about twenty years.

But I'd also taken a bona fide cross-country walk once, and my memories of the trek gave me a sense of belonging—a false one, since walking guys excluded me from their club as soon as they learned the route I took.

My present company was no exception. "North to south?" he repeated, making sure he hadn't misheard.

According to the standard measure, that didn't count. It lacked the commitment and totality of coast-to-coast—unless you hiked the entirety of the Appalachian Trail or the Continental Divide. Enjoyment was not the point, only the completion of some macho ritual as a rite.

As we talked, I thought: "There's something about this dude that's off." I realized I'd been blinded by his shtick. He might easily be a murderer, a nut, or worse: a norm, a bore, a waste of time. Being a walking guy didn't vouch for his character; in fact, it covered it up. Like joining the French Foreign Legion, it was a package deal that granted you a new persona, cause, and dubious goal.

Then it struck me: so did moving here—and don't get me started on the natives. When it came to leaning on a myth to make your life meaningful, New Yorkers were even worse than walking guys, and touched by the same madness. Our superiority complex is off the charts, without ever braving the elements or earning a blister. That exceptionalism made the guy beside me seem comparatively sane.

2

"Why are you whispering?" Mary asked.

"I'm on assignment," I said. "Investigating a fake walking guy on the west side."

"Are you in danger? Most walking guys are nuts."

"You think so?"

"Definitely. My eighth-grade teacher. My dad, kind of. You. Even Evo Morales, although I'm a fan. Isn't one of your friends a walking guy, too?"

"Yes, Ian. That's why I'm calling. Can you pull out the noose in my desk drawer and read me the number on it? Don't worry, it's just a memento from his walk. It's crazy, the stuff you find on the side of the road."

I could hear her shudder over the phone. Or so I thought. Actually, it was a computerized voice cutting us off: "Continue south on footpath. In approximately one hundred feet, veer slightly to the left."

I gasped in horror and was about to dash the borrowed device on the rocks when the walking guy intervened. He'd been leaning on the nearby railing, striking a Whitmanesque pose as he gazed meaningfully toward Lady Liberty. Now he beamed a beatific, bemused look at the phone. "My guide," he purred. "It led me all the way across this great land."

If the modern world was bad, a modern seeker-slash-sage was worse. Fucking 'walking guy dot com.' Suddenly I realized the journals he'd been keeping were live.

"We're on the waterfront," I growled. "It's a grid, like Iowa. There's only one direction to go—unless you choose to turn back."

My last words had an immediate effect, as I knew they would. While he was momentarily stunned, I ducked into a bathroom and dialed fast. "Ian," I said, "meet me on the West Side Highway ay-sap, sporting walking-guy camp."

If anything, Ian overdid the role. Before long, he appeared coming towards us. He was carrying a staff, decked out in seventies-style shorts and a Vietnamese peasant hat. A massive backpack and bedroll rose behind his head like the sun.

"Wow," my companion sighed.

"Go in peace," I told him. "I feel my life's journey

has changed course." I joined Ian quickly and we headed north.

In our wake, the walking guy clasped his hands and made a small bow. "Namaste."

3

"Thanks, man," I told Ian. "That was starting to feel like crossing Texas again."

He smiled, dimples showing underneath the conical hat. "It's nice to help someone on the road, even if they're only on a day trip. So many people helped me when I was on my walk."

I had called Ian not just for pest control purposes, but because I considered him an expert on the subject at hand. He was my closest, and perhaps only, walking-guy friend.

I asked him for a full debriefing, including tips on how to distinguish phony walking guys from the real thing, so that he wouldn't need to rescue me again. But he dismissed that distinction out of hand.

"There are two kinds of artists," he explained. "People who can't function in society in any normal way—and everybody else. With walking guys, it's the same.

"I made the decision to turn away from society and start walking, but I ran into guys out there who were constitutionally *incapable* of integrating, the same way punks run into real hobos when they're riding freight trains. They admire the hobos and maybe don't notice that they're not drinking for the same reason, even if it looks the same on the surface."

I asked: "How' about westbound walking guys versus those headed the other way?" I was razzing him a bit, since Ian was the only member of the former group.

"The difference," he said, "is that eastbound guys probably thought it out in advance. Going east, you have the wind at your back. Going west, you're walking into the wind the entire way.

"But that's part of it, too: Sometimes you have to be shit out of luck. It rained thirty of my first thirty-two days. My feet were so rotten, and I had poison ivy from New Jersey until past the Mississippi.

"And maybe that speaks to the essence of the walking guy. If someone knows how to avoid discomfort, that's not a walking guy. You didn't ask about the guys who think they're Jesus, but I can tell you were leading up to it.

"Here's the thing, though: you're going to be hard pressed to find Jesus out on the open road. On the edge of town, sure, lots of them—but always heading back in. Those are *talking* guys, not walking guys. The crazy guy or messianic guy is looking for attention, and he's not going to last a week out there walking. It's too lonely and dull.

"But I wouldn't say that one is on the level and one is not, because my kind of walking guy looks up to the other kind—and I think that kind of walking guy also admired mine.

"I probably have more in common with the walking guy you just ditched than you'd like to think. He might be an annoying guy, but I'm an annoying guy, too. Being annoying may be a prerequisite for being a walking guy. You need a certain kind of obliviousness, and the stubbornness to push on even though it's ridiculous."

Ian's words humbled me and brought me back to my own walking days: the expansive sense of freedom, and the enormous chip on my shoulder that came with it. If not a messianic complex, it was certainly a superiority trip.

The other side of the coin was just as bad. It seemed impossible to be a city guy—a sitting guy—without becoming a bit of a dismissive jerk.

I remembered thinking of the city as a rat race filled with stressed-out people chasing their own tails. I vowed not to lose perspective when I waded back in, but of course I did. The skyline disappears from view as you became part of it.

Luckily, I had Ian to remind me that walking is like other forms of recovery. There's no such thing as a former walking guy. It'll always be part of you.

Bent Stories

THE SHOW at Jane Doe Books is a disappointing one. Ian slips out the door while no one is looking, feeling depressed. A Cinco de Mayo celebration is taking place outside one of the Montrose Avenue bars, and he watches wide-eyed. Arriving home in a haze, Ian finds me on the Bent House roof, waiting for the sunrise.

"I sure wish I could dance like those guys," he sighs.

2

Ren wakes me up, anxious to talk. "I've been to temple already three times this month," he confesses.

Clearly this story is about a girl, so I cut to the chase. "She's not some religious nut, is she? Don't tell me she actually believes in God."

"No," Ren says, "she doesn't. But I do."

"That's different."

"How so?" He points his beard at me ponderously.

"Because you're crazy, and we love you for it. But stay away from those religious folks—they're *actually* crazy. It's a whole different ballpark."

3

I've always explained my friends in terms of different distortion pedals. If only they would turn down the effects I'd be able to understand what the hell they're trying to say.

But I never made the obvious connection: all my friends are guitarists. They're used to communicating through a bunch of filters. The more I thought about it, the more it made sense. No such problem with drummers—they're clear enough.

I called up Skip. We sat on the old loading dock at Toxic Swamp pitching pebbles into the sputtering, bubbling water.

"Life sucks," I said. But he looked at me and shook his head.

4

Perhaps we had begun walking together at the kinetic sculpture race many years before. We had begun running at Petra's funeral. It was all too much, a sinking feeling of being pinned down by grief. We looked at one another and just took off at a clip, tearing down the hill in our fancy funeral clothes, a crazy pile of punks running down the middle of the road.

We kept it up after that, twice a week, just to keep our blood moving and stay one step ahead of the doom. Sometimes Skip, Ian, or Ren would join us, but mostly it was a private thing, Jamie and I yelling about our problems and worries until they started to feel a little ridiculous, panting while we lapped around the track at McCarren Park.

One week a voice came from the bushes, making us jump. "Will you guys shut up already? Some of us need to sleep."

5

My first girlfriend was tortured. A tortured young poet. Late at night when the businesses were all closed up, the tourists tucked into their beds in San Jose, and even the monarch butterflies headed south for the season, my tortured ex-girlfriend would take crosstops and skate down to the big cliff on the beach, and there she would sit, perched as if ready to take flight, cold but not caring, composing poems.

She sent them to me and I returned them edited, with the lines I didn't like crossed out. I was actually that much of a jerk.

Recently she called me up. "I was listening to 'Stick Around' off the first Bent album," she said, "and I thought of you."

6

It was so cold on the Bent House roof, I couldn't do any handwriting. I climbed down, turned on the kitchen light, and sat on the counter rolling a smoke. Just then, a blinding flash flared up in the distance. All the lights in the city went dead. I took a drag—the only spark left in town. Now I couldn't do any handwriting at all. Nothing to do but crack open a beer and freeze. With no power, everyone in town would be just as cold as me up on the Bent House roof. That was a comforting thought.

The door swung open. I pulled on the smoke, drawing just enough light to recognize the Chasid from the flower warehouse downstairs who always stopped by wanting to play Skip's drums. He stood in the doorway with a pair of sticks and an eager look in his eye. Well, why not? While he banged away at the kit in the darkness I nibbled on the rugelach he'd brought, trying to read by the light of the moon.

7

Jamie called and said, "Why don't you come along? There's five pairs of brass knuckles and only four of us."

Put that way, how could I refuse? I love a good, bloody fight. But what band would be stupid enough to take me on tour?

When we broke down on the side of the road in Oklahoma, I laughed. Right in Ren's face, fogging up his glasses. But Ren just smiled back.

The fuel pump was shot to hell and the fan belt was in pieces, littering the road like confetti. My kind of party. Someone had even invited the cops.

"This is nice," said Skip, usually the grumpy one of the bunch. "For a cruel joke, it's pretty funny."

Ian chimed in. "Even if it is dark and this is the scariest place I've ever been and we'll definitely miss the show tonight, we could all use a little walk. So I guess it's for the best."

I groaned. I love a good breakdown, I even love their band, but this was unbearable. I motioned for a new rule and it passed unanimously: no more making the best out of a bad situation. No optimistic lessons learned from disasters—at least not in the first hour. Yet not five minutes later, Ren was talking again.

"I'm not trying to be optimistic or anything," he said. "But at least we're still a band. That's important, right?"

8

Unabomber wakes up, rubs his blurry eyes. He cracks some eggs into the frying pan and kicks around the cabin looking for the salt. What a mess it all is. Can't throw anything away, not even a shopping list, lest someone find it and use it against you. So what happens? It all stacks up, of course. The piles grown into mountains that devour even the salt. He curses, but what's the use? Just eat your tasteless eggs and get on with it.

Unabomber has the day off. No more having to answer to the foreman at the mill, he can set his own rules today. Ride into town, grab some coffee and a new ribbon for the rusty old typer. Best of all, he can spend the whole afternoon in the luxury of the library. Not literal luxury, but the kind no money can buy.

Knowledge, the most glorious and beautiful of all the world's riches. Priceless—and free, as we should all be.

It's the day before New Year's, his last chance to check out books this year. Unabomber parks his bike and strolls inside. He settles into his regular spot, deciding on a whim to reread Thoreau. Seeing him there, the librarian waves hello. Her most loyal customer! Is there a slight crush at work, or just a natural fondness between two lovers of literature? Either way, for him she sets aside the library's out-of-date magazines rather than throwing them away. From these, he selects targets—but how could she guess such a thing? And how is he to know that in the year since these magazines first arrived, the chairman of ITT and the vice president of Boeing have both relocated, moving into even larger and more commanding offices, leaving their old digs to be taken over by a Starbucks and a bagel place?

Well, that's the breaks. A sad day for the shlemazel at Boomer Bagels but a lucky day for the VP of Boeing who gets to keep on living, making his own bombs, a crime for which *he'll* never have to face the death penalty.

Jamie nudges me, ending my five minutes in the limelight. He's done changing his broken string, so I step off the stage leaving my allegorical story unfinished. Not that the audience notices or cares. Four pimply kids in Sioux Falls—for this we drove across the Great Plains? Behind me Ren launches into "Starin' at the Walls." Touring can be a real heartbreaker at times.

9

I had one hand on the bike and one hand on Skip. Nothing like a little motorcycle ride to refresh yourself and shake off the static. Weaving in and out of traffic, slicing a line right through the lights and wind and noise. It makes you feel sharp and decisive even when you're not.

We were on the bridge when I felt my tuque start to slip. Too late to save it, the hat went flying off into traffic like a drunken bat. Shoot. Nothing like losing your hat to make you feel unfocused, out of place, and unsure of yourself. The opposite of a motorcycle. But Skip yelled back over the roar of the engine. "No problem," he said. "I've got fifty just like it at home."

Fifty? No kidding. I'd been dreaming of buying fifty black hats, fifty little white undershirts, and fifty toothbrushes just as a precautionary measure. A whole closet full of security blankets, so to speak.

"I've got the closet full and under the bed too," yelled Skip. He executed a hairpin turn and nearly delivered us to an early death. "You can help yourself," he said, then explained before I had a chance to ask. All he said was one word. That was enough to get the whole story and a good laugh.

Everyone has a few words like that, code names for amazing plans they had and the subsequent devastating failure and wholesale slaughter of those amazing plans. Be it a house, a romance, a road trip, a business venture, or—for Skip—a band, those words all at once sum up your biggest expectations and sharpest disappointments. Aiming too high and landing too low.

We laugh. That's life—ironic, unfair. But in our world it's rarely bad luck or lack of support that brings on the doom. Riding through the wreckage of my friends' lives, I can see well-placed wrenches stuck in the works, perhaps even glimpse someone shooting themselves in the foot. Everyone likes to know that they tried, and usually that they failed and can stop trying now.

I call it the ninety-nine percent success story. The noble failure. Hundreds of novels lie completed but not published, albums recorded but not pressed, tours booked but then hastily cancelled, articles written but never sent. Vast and impressive castles are built, but they're not inhabitable. Just one nail in the right place and we could move in, but I show up with a hammer and they block my way. "Not yet," they say.

Why is everyone so scared to put in the last one percent? They've gone through the pains of labor, yet can't bear to see their child leave the nest. They've sown the seed, but let the fruit rot on the tree. (And it's not just because my girlfriend is pregnant and I've been helping Mary on the farm that I'm thinking in those terms.)

Skip had ordered clothes, burned the screens, and bought the ink, but somehow never got around to putting the ingredients together. None of my business, you might say, but I disagree. That closet full of clean clothes is a reminder of an unfinished, unfulfilled promise that Skip made to himself. As a community it's our duty to try to bring everyone's ambitious plans to fruition instead of passively watching and encouraging that potential to be wasted. To keep laughing, but keep the hard work and hope that comes with it from becoming a joke. As a friend, it's my duty to try to be that missing piece, that one percent.

Skip and I ended up crashing the bike that night— on a residential street, not the BQE. He couldn't decide which way to turn, and my screaming didn't help. Skip flew over the handlebars but was only slightly scratched, passing it off with a characteristic shrug.

In the excitement, and the exhaustion of working together to lift the bike and roll it home, I forgot to help myself to one of Skip's hats. Fifty of them just sitting there gathering dust. It burns me up to think about it every time I lose another one.

10

Johnny Hell was a city punk, with a mohawk and a basement apartment exiting into the parking lot of one of San Francisco's most exclusive restaurants, where the valet parkers lived in fear of Johnny's spikes, studs, and rambunctious moods. I accepted this picture at face value, even becoming part of it on occasion when we would chase each other home, hopping from hood to hood on the expensive cars.

Who would have guessed that Johnny Hell was really the punk kingpin of Salt Lake City, where he still lived, and that little Leroy Newman was just some nebbish who'd stolen Johnny's name and image lock, stock, and barrel when he moved to San Francisco? Not I, too naive at the time to consider that people aren't always who they present themselves to be. Similarly, Bob didn't really have cancer as he claimed, and Chalky the bassist of my old band turned out to be a sociopath with a different name and wardrobe for each of his split personalities. The blue hair he wouldn't let anyone touch turned out to be—you guessed it—a wig, though it was six months before we figured it out. Imagine how his girlfriend Justine felt!

I stumbled through the Bent House with the blues, thinking about all the fakes I'd known through the years. Was it ever possible to know anyone for real? We were all still trying out different roles. But when did roleplaying cross the line into dishonesty?

Sunshine filtered through the greasy windows, bathing the Bent boys in a hazy light as they lay scattered on the floor. I looked at each of them in turn, troubled by old thoughts of identity and truth. Who were they trying to be? And who were they really?

11

The party where we first met was on Myrtle Avenue in Brooklyn, at the apartment Petra and Yvette shared. An angry band was playing. The guitarist leaned smoking against the wall as he played, drunkenly unaware that in fact it was you he was leaning on.

Pinned between the guitarist and the wall, you smiled a feeble, embarrassed smile. Our eyes met, yet I was unable to save you. I made faces, flailing my arms as a signal to Jamie, but it was no use. I'd already been yelling, flailing, and making faces all night, filling in for Bent's regular drummer, Skip. Exaggerating the gestures only made me appear to be rocking out, which in turn caused Jamie to lean further back in drunken guitarist ecstasy. To pry him off would've meant stopping the song in the middle, which not only seemed a shame, it was against the Ten Commandments of the band. Instead I played harder and faster, hoping for a quick and merciful end.

Being the last band at the party is always awkward. Once you've built up the tension into explosion and release, everyone turns around and leaves. For a singer it's not so bad, but with drums you can't just walk away. By the time I'd broken down the kit and packed up, you were gone.

There were only four people left in the living room. Petra was under Jamie's spell as he showed off three sheets of acid, a hundred hits each. Yvette was in the corner with Ian swapping spit, but when I came in to say goodbye she insisted on walking me to the subway.

The G train is supposed to run every twenty minutes, but enraged passengers had crossed out "minutes" and written "hours" or "years" on most signs. On that bench with Yvette, time slowed to a crawl. She had powerful lips that spoke of self-assurance and certainty. A kiss never tastes as good as when it knows it will be followed by a farewell, but it's rare you get a full session in—a good taste. Not without missing your train and messing up the whole thing. But timing turned out to be another of Yvette's perfections.

I sat on the G train tunneling through Bed-Stuy in a happy daze. I smiled, wondering and laughing at life. I stayed on all the way to Greenpoint, on a hunch that Fake Pink Awning would be open and I'd find my friends there—old friends from my extremely short-lived art school days.

Sure enough, they were there. Three in the morning on a Thursday. Life was good. I slumped down in a hard plastic booth next to Zippo and Ruth, laughing hysterically.

"What's so funny?" they asked. "And why are you all red?"

Oh shit. Now I remembered. When Jamie wasn't looking I'd grabbed one of his sheets of acid and jokingly taken a lick.

12

Volatile is Ian's word of the day. Changing rapidly under pressure. Ephemeral, fleeting, explosive and tending to erupt. Fits on his knuckles like Phil Ochs, and one more dumb tattoo can't hurt. "Moody" is for hippies, "Pensive" for poets. Leave him with the explosives.

Okay, so he's moody and pensive too. But he's learned his lessons about being self-contained and knowing when to hold your cards. Now when he sees an old friend on the street he just nods. It's what you don't tell, and don't have to explain, that really resonates. "Notes not played," as Skip says.

So why this friction, this combustibility today? He tries to shrug it off but can't. Well, we all have to break character sometime. He looks it up. Volatile, from the Latin *volare*: to fly.

I'll just coast on this for a while, he decides.

13

A misunderstanding between friends led to an argument, and the argument led to a certain Russian-born guitarist getting kicked out onto the street. That led, invariably, to my door, where Ren showed up at 1:00 a.m. looking for some comforting words and a less comfortable bed.

"Poor Ren," I said.

"Could you say that again, please?" he asked.

"Poor Ren. Poor downtrodden thing. Poor wretched, wrecked little Ren. Poor dismal, fucked-up little guy. Rotting, sad, stepped on Ren. Into my arms with you."

Though he was no longer a scrawny kid, I managed to cradle Ren and rock him back and forth, rubbing his head in my big hands.

After years of discussing and debating problems, I'd learned the value of a little tender, unconditional sympathy instead.

14

For instance, I was on the back of a motorcycle curled up to the most beautiful girl in the world. Steam was rising off the streams on both sides of us as we flew down the dirt road in the early morning cold. I had my hands in the pockets of her leather jacket, in a trance-like state of bliss. And then? Well, use your imagination.

Or Heidi and I hopping trains. Huddled up and listening to the rhythm of the clickety-clacking tracks, we watched the redwoods as they passed. My first-ever time hopping trains. But what happened the second time? And who is Heidi? None of your goddam business.

My point is this: the end of the story isn't always the most important part. It might not even be part of the story at all, depending on how you choose to tell it. I'm sick of walking around with friends talking about ends—the ends of relationships, friendships, feelings, and hope. We all know how things end, and that's badly. But just because it came last, it need not overshadow everything else. If you lived it, it's all part of the story of your life—or in this case, the story of your band—and it can be added up and remembered in many different ways. We could trade in all our hopeful beginnings and buy a yacht and a summer home. We could trade in all the bitter ends for a warm bottle of beer. Either way, I'm thankful that most of us are still here.

Seventh & Flatbush News
(As Told by the Wandering Eye)

THE HAT GUY is on his way out after forty years in his doorless cave on the corner, where he braves the elements till late at night peddling the sorts of wares once known as five-and-dime. No awning has he, no sign, just a perch next to a roll gate and what might pass for a firehouse garage, narrow and long. I admire him greatly, for he calmly and kindly holds his post while exchanging endearments with almost everyone who passes, whether young children, old dowagers, or recently escaped convicts. He does not pander, but presents himself with such honesty that everyone's indifference dissolves into an easy warmth.

What will he do with his time, I ask. "Farm," he replies. Does he have a plot at one of the nearby community gardens? The city, after all, is full of folks with delusional plans to raise livestock in their apartment or do subsistence farming on the roof.

But the Hat Guy laughs. "I have eight hundred acres upstate," he informs me, enjoying watching my jaw drop. Not for nothing has he been toiling away on this busy corner for decades, it turns out. "A field of soybeans," he says. "A field of ginseng. A full-size basketball court."

The Hat Guy has been biding his time and banking his cash and soon will be a back-to-the-lander—though no tent or yurt for him. He's been going up in the winter and building for his future all along. Now there are seven houses, one for him and one for each of his kids. Yet the idle life is not in the cards even when he leaves his present digs. "I'll still be doing some import-export," he says. "Forty years I've been in this country, but I still have connections in Seoul."

Yes, he's bought the farm, and will soon be plowing the land if only the Hat Kid will pay the rest of the agreed price. Only a down payment has thus far been made, and there's been some difficulties shaking down the rest of what's due. The Hat Kid—no youngster but still a novice in comparison—is a native of the neighborhood looking for his own retirement plan, but his salary as a cop has been undermined by too many dependents.

And so the Hat Guy waits, patient as the Sphinx, selling me socks which are not as one-size-fits-all as the package claims.

Socks are one thing, shoes another matter indeed. Sad to say, though the Hat Guy plans to leave, the speedier departure from our beloved corner has come unannounced and, I fear, unplanned. That's right: too-small socks are all we have to protect our feet now that the cobbler has fled the scene.

He was a beloved figure himself, and since his shoe shop wasn't far from Cobble Hill, I affectionately referred to the place as Cobbler Hell. The place was a dingy, shoe-box/matchbox-sized shop with a "Give racism the boot" poster and yellow clippings on the wall. A dusty menorah sat in one corner, and on the counter an oversized can with the scrawled inscription of a drowning man. "Tips—for coffee!" it read. Closer inspection showed that it was attached to the counter by a very large string to thwart those who might take it to go.

Ah, there's more, much more, all on this one little corner of Brooklyn. But let's pause and pour a drop of coffee first for our departed friends.

Seventh & Flatbush News Issue #2

Somebody stole my bike. Hardly a newsworthy item, I realize, in a city where every bike thief is a master craftsmen with a blowtorch and a can of liquid nitrogen on their tool belt.

But this is an unusual case. To start with, it was missing a seat. What's more, I'd stopped bothering to lock it up, due to the construction crews whose round-the-clock digging has left our once-lovely streets looking like 1982 Beirut. Ostensibly they are installing a new sewer main, but more likely they are on a rage parade, randomly laying waste to anything in their path. Before giving up on my lock I'd twice found my bike still chained up where I'd left it, but with the pole I'd attached it to nowhere in sight.

As Marx said, "You have nothing to lose but your

chains." Turns out he was wrong, but I took his advice and threw mine away. I leaned my Schwinn against a tree. It was free. Locked or not, it remained in front of my lid until earlier this eve.

When I found it gone, I felt a stinging sense of loss. True, the Schwinn wasn't a very functional ride, but it was a stand-in—an urban version of the horse in the pasture that greeted me every time I came home.

Feeling forlorn, I headed down to our Thieves Market, that stretch of Seventh Avenue where all and sundry is hawked by enterprising ragpickers. Yet there was no rusty red frame to be seen, only several scratched Seals and Crofts LPs, the measly inheritance for those of us who showed up in Park Slope too late to claim a rent-controlled pad.

Without a clear plan, I headed to the corner to find comfort at the crossroads. Everyone makes an appearance at Flatbush and Seventh if you wait long enough. It's our village square, our Penny Lane, where you can watch the people, waving to those you know and wondering about those you don't.

I gazed across the four lanes of traffic as if across a mighty river. The flow of cars was steady but not particularly soothing. The other shore, where video and thrift stores once stood, seemed impossibly far.

Soon the sky clouded over and snow began to fall. That fit my melancholy mood, for it was not just my steed that was missing, but the Grill Guy as well.

Maybe you remember him? He stood in the back of the seedy smoke shop that was tucked between the

Hat Guy and Cobbler Hell. The store was dark and foreboding like me, yet when I stepped inside I still felt ill at ease. Every bodega is staffed by guys whose aggressive sarcasm is hard to take, but at this joint they were extra cutting. Though I grind myself day and night—mostly night—upon the whetstone of New York, I'm still hardly razor sharp.

The fact is, it was easier to walk up Flatbush to the yuppie greengrocer with the ingratiating manner that came from being afraid of getting bad Yelp reviews. One more battle for the real neighborhood character of the city, and I voted against it, I'm ashamed to admit.

Yet some instinct kept me returning periodically to the smoke shop. Maybe I wanted to prove myself by refusing to be driven away. Maybe I could sense that their antagonism was a front—a hard shell protecting a soft spot.

When I did finally make it past the register, what I found was impossibly sweet: a long lunch counter at least a century old, tucked into the back wall, totally invisible from the street. There was no sign to lure customers in, yet the place was packed, with only one stool free.

Manning the grill was a soft-spoken Palestinian with a tough but motherly manner. "Come here anytime," he told me. "You don't need to buy anything, just sit. I'm here all night."

And so I did.

Everything changes, but when change came to our little corner, it came fast and caught me off guard. First, the Hat Guy started talking about buying the farm. Then the wry devil from Cobbler Hell simply disappeared. When it seemed like nothing more could go wrong, I walked down to the Grill for a burger and some kind words and found the place boarded up. The Grill Guy was gone.

They'd taken my whole band—even our roadie, the cobbler's shepherd-looking son. Now you can understand why, when they stole my bike too, I took it so hard.

Where can you go for solace when the place you went for solace is gone? For once, that existential question was easy to answer, because a bustling city corner resembles a small town in at least one regard: there are only a few plots from which to choose. With the Grill cold and closed, I had to relocate. Now you can find me at Ruby Kitchen next door.

The cook here is less effusive, but the atmosphere is casual and the food affordable, and that's close enough. Life may get worse every year, but you make up the difference by being better at coping with it. That's the deal, or at least the ideal. You work with what you've got.

I sat at the window sipping wonton soup and watching the glistening flakes of snow drift from the sky. And then I spotted it, parked right outside: my Schwinn! Some hoarder had added it to their tangle of busted bikes, our corner's version of modern art.

I leapt on my steed, preparing to ride it home. But it was locked.

Everyone has been asking, "Eye, what do you make of the new park they've installed on the corner made famous by your reports?" They want to know if the remodel is a warning sign or just another odd choice from City Planning, like the oversized flowerpot blocking pedestrians further up the block.

A true gathering point like Washington Square it is not, only a traffic island with ringside seats to huff exhaust. But anything less than a total loss is cause for celebration these days, so take a seat and kick up your feet. That's what I've done. I sat there all through the unusually warm winter, gazing out across the main artery of our neighborhood, the raging river on whose banks we've built our lives.

Smoking? Drinking? Barbecuing? None of the above. Simply trying to see to the other side.

I was responding to charges of favoritism in the form of graffiti penned on the wall of Ruby Kitchen, accusing me of focusing solely on the eastern side of the intersection that this newsletter—and my heart—is dedicated to.

The worst part was that they were absolutely true. The *other* Flatbush and Seventh is almost completely unknown to me, with its rival Chinese restaurant, phone company, and pharmacy. It's a bizarro version of the institutions I patronize every day—a distorted, funhouse-mirror image of the corner I call home. And

I can't help but feel like it's casting aspersions and thumbing its nose.

Crazy as it may seem, the vast gulf between the two corners isn't only in my mind. Flatbush is the border between two neighborhoods, with different city councilmembers and different zip codes on opposing shores. The other side may as well be another country, with a DMZ in the middle that you take your life in your hands trying to traverse.

As a result, my trips to the west side of Flatbush and Seventh have been mostly by accident. Even a native New Yorker occasionally gets turned around and takes the wrong subway exit.

On a recent rainy afternoon I sat in Ruby Kitchen pondering the matter. Most of the local movers and shakers were present, just like at the Grill before they got rid of the tables and rebranded the place "Best and Quick Gourmet."

The Incense Guy sat in a corner with shades and headphones on. I'm pretty sure he knows every secret in the neighborhood—including my name—from the discarded letters he peruses while digging in the trash for cans. But he never gives them away. He keeps his own company even in a crowd, like the homeless guy who sleeps in Meadowport Arch in Prospect Park and overhears the conversations of all who pass.

In earlier installments of this newsletter, I visited shop owners when there was a mystery to solve. The Hat Guy knew where everyone on Flatbush had come from and escaped to without ever leaving his pedestal-like perch. The cobbler at Cobbler Hell was always quick with a quip for which I was the punch line.

But lately I've been trying to be more like the Incense Guy and search for clues instead of approval and advice. I practice the power of deduction. I try to look inscrutable. Including the mystery man I was apprenticing, the suspects around me were quite usual, relatively speaking. At Ruby, if nowhere else, they were considered regular.

Bread Dread slurped soup at her table. My fashion-conscious friends call her the "Princess of Plaza Street," referring to the promenade leading towards Prospect Park which is alternately known as the Teardrop, the Tangent, or the Berms.

Next to her, perched on adjacent stools by the window, were three sworn foes. The first was the teenager who tags his moniker on local walls. The second, the muttering middle-aged obsessive who roams the streets in the dead of night covering up graffiti with house paint. Last was the art school lass who adds faces to his pastel strokes, changing them into cute animal portraits.

The trio provided each other with a sense of purpose, not to mention a regular workout. But they were totally unaware of each other's identities, because each thought themselves cleverer and more invisible than they really are. But then, so do we all.

That was the beauty of our little corner of the world. Here, people overlooked or looked down upon elsewhere were legendary all-stars playing together on the same team. Sometimes when the sun was high in the sky and I was sitting on the bench, I'd picture the crosswalks of Flatbush forming a baseball diamond, with Pastel Brush at first and the Hat Guy pitching a no-run game.

No doubt, our intersection is its own ecosystem. It certainly doesn't function as a doorman or red carpet for the two neighborhoods it fronts. More like a scar on their face, or a zit—a reminder of younger and rougher days.

At times like this when the weather forced us inside, it was easier to imagine everyone as the band I was trying to reform. Bread Dread was on bass, natch, and the art student was the guitarist always threatening to leave and start a solo career. I was working up the nerve to ask the preteen child of the Ruby Kitchen fry cook if he wanted to sing.

But who would fill out the group now that the cobbler from Cobbler Hell had fled Flatbush, along with his solemn, shepherd-like cobbler kid?

Taking a chance, I tore out the door and ran through the pelting rain. I was headed for the dreaded other side with a burning suspicion in my mind.

Not only was there a different Chinese restaurant on the other shore, but faces staring out its window that looked just as strange as ours. Yet I'd spotted something else: a mirror image of the shop our side had recently lost, with the same sign offering hastily copied keys that only work half the time.

I almost tore the little bell off the door as I blew inside.

Sure enough, a wisecracking Uzbeki Jew stood behind the counter hammering crazily on an errant heel—a perfect stand-in for the cobbler I knew.

"A drummer, by chance?" I asked.

He grinned devilishly. "You got my note."

Soup

SKIP ALWAYS started stories, but he could never finish them. My file cabinets were full of his rough drafts, novels he wasn't able to move past the opening scenes. Our conversations were the same: promising but unresolved and anticlimactic. Then, one night, as we sat in the dingy back corner of Yonah Schimmel huddled over two bowls of soup, the solution to his impasse revealed itself. "From now on," Skip announced, "every story ends like this."

When I asked him to articulate, he waved his arms around. "Like this. Watch, I'll show you.

"Ever hear about the time me and Katie from Haiti hotwired a motorcycle and drove it all the way to Denver? We get there finally and she can't stop laughing. What's so funny, I want to know. She laughs so hard she wets her pants. 'It's my boyfriend's bike,' she says. 'And he's a cop.'"

"And then?" I asked.

"And then I walked into Yonah Schimmel and had matzoh ball soup with Aaron. The end."

"That's it?"

"You want more? Okay, Aaron took the seat by

the back so he could watch the ladies pass by on their way to the bathroom while pretending to give me his undivided attention. I was stuck in the seat facing the mirror, and Christ did I need a shave. 'Add a side of latkes,' I told the waitress when she came around with the check."

"With sour cream or applesauce?"

"Both."

It was a comforting thought. The one recurring ritual in our lives that was never anything but soothing, calming, and sweet, repeated endlessly. We sat across the table facing each other yet having a hard time believing that two losers could ever get so lucky. I shook my head. "It can't be that easy."

"It can and it is. My books will soon be rolling off the presses, one after another."

As his editor I was hopeful but skeptical. "Try again."

"Okay, I'm in the car with Mom. Some crazy guy is driving. Angry, Irish, a total asshole. They should make guys go through mandatory counseling before they have unprotected sex. For the sake of brevity, let's call him 'Dad.' But wait, just when you think you've heard this one before, there's a catch.

"We're driving through Central Park—I must have been nine or ten at the time—and just as we come to a red light, this wild hippie sticks his head through the back window and looks me right in the eye. 'Nanook, no no,' he says. I finish the sentence: 'Don't be a naughty Eskimo.' But just to myself, not out loud.

"The hippie is already gone, bouncing down the road. It happened so fast that my parents didn't even notice, but I may as well have been struck by lightning. You know that revelation—the first time you realize, 'There are others like me out there!'

"Now it seems ridiculous. Of course someone else had heard Frank Zappa, probably alone in their room, spinning the dial of their radio the same way I did. But you think everything is a private, secret thing when you're a kid—a message only you've received."

I took Skip's pause as my cue to cut in. "Let me guess, thirty years later you walk into a Jewish deli. 'Ever wonder what happened to that hippie?' your editor asks, smiling mischievously.

"Looking him over, you have to admit, there's a resemblance. But it's impossible. Thirty years ago, he couldn't have had a beard—or could he?

"Before you're able to ask, something stops you. It's that delicious sense of mystery. You pick up the spoon instead and dip into the bowl of matzoh ball soup that's just been served. Yellow and glistening with fatty drops of oil, it's the only sustenance and light in the lives of this pair of aging punks—the only thing that keeps them alive and able to meet, as they do, once or even twice a week.

"The end. Okay, Skip, you've proved it—your model works. But you said there was a catch. That, I don't see."

Skip smiled. "Neither do I, yet. But there's got to be a catch. What am I supposed to do, spend my whole life in Brooklyn, taking the train to work at some shitty theater, then meeting you for matzoh ball soup? Well, I hope so. What more could I want? It's a great life."

Easy to say, and nice to hear. But when Skip's long-lost love got back in touch, that was all it took. One month later he'd quit his job, packed up, and moved to Wyoming, never to be seen again. Not even the old unfinished stories in the mail. Goodbye, dear friend— without you it's just not the same.

And then? If nothing else, he'd left me with a happy ending that never changed. We sat in the back of Yonah Schimmel, so happy we could cry just to be together. Steam rose from two bowls of soup, getting cold while their owners lost themselves in each other's stories.

ABOUT PM PRESS

PM Press is an independent, radical publisher of critically necessary books for our tumultuous times. Our aim is to deliver bold political ideas and vital stories to all walks of life and arm the dreamers to demand the impossible. Founded in 2007 by a small group of people with decades of publishing, media, and organizing experience, we have sold millions of copies of our books, most often one at a time, face to face. We're old enough to know what we're doing and young enough to know what's at stake. Join us to create a better world.

PM Press
PO Box 23912
Oakland, CA 94623
www.pmpress.org

PM Press in Europe
europe@pmpress.org
www.pmpress.org.uk

FRIENDS OF PM PRESS

These are indisputably momentous times—the financial system is melting down globally and the Empire is stumbling. Now more than ever there is a vital need for radical ideas.

In the many years since its founding—and on a mere shoestring—PM Press has risen to the formidable challenge of publishing and distributing knowledge and entertainment for the struggles ahead. With hundreds of releases to date, we have published an impressive and stimulating array of literature, art, music, politics, and culture. Using every available medium, we've succeeded in connecting those hungry for ideas and information to those putting them into practice.

Friends of PM allows you to directly help impact, amplify, and revitalize the discourse and actions of radical writers, filmmakers, and artists. It provides us with a stable foundation from which we can build upon our early successes and provides a much-needed subsidy for the materials that can't necessarily pay their own way. You can help make that happen—and receive every new title automatically delivered to your door once a month—by joining as a Friend of PM Press. And, we'll throw in a free T-shirt when you sign up.

Here are your options:
- **$30 a month** Get all books and pamphlets plus a 50% discount on all webstore purchases
- **$40 a month** Get all PM Press releases (including CDs and DVDs) plus a 50% discount on all webstore purchases
- **$100 a month** Superstar—Everything plus PM merchandise, free downloads, and a 50% discount on all webstore purchases

For those who can't afford $30 or more a month, we have **Sustainer Rates** at $15, $10 and $5. Sustainers get a free PM Press T-shirt and a 50% discount on all purchases from our website.

Your Visa or Mastercard will be billed once a month, until you tell us to stop. Or until our efforts succeed in bringing the revolution around. Or the financial meltdown of Capital makes plastic redundant. Whichever comes first.

The Loneliness of the Electric Menorah

Aaron Cometbus

ISBN: 979-8-88744-063-7
$12.95   160 pages

In 1963 the paperback revolution was making good literature widely available for the first time, yet only a handful of stores took the trend seriously enough to devote themselves to the cause. Rambam, a closet-sized shop on a corner of Berkeley's Telegraph Avenue was one.

The owners had a falling out, as partners often do, but the results were glorious instead of tragic, with ripples that birthed much of the culture we take for granted now. Underground comics, New Age publishing, used record stores, and poster art all came from Rambam's big bang, as each new business with visionary (but ornery) partners formed and then split again.

The Loneliness of the Electric Menorah is the social history of one of America's most legendary streets, and a family tree of the movements it fostered: the paperback revolution, the graphic novel, Slow Food, New Age, the Free Speech Movement—and even the Symbionese Liberation Army.

"Cometbus is no navel-gazer. He questions what community is, over and over, in different ways—angrily or jokingly, but always with a sober and informed wit."
—SF Weekly